HEAD TO HEAD

To Neil
ALL my love
your Dorcas
xx

SMITH&JONES
HEADTOHEAD

Fontana
An Imprint of HarperCollinsPublishers

Fontana
An Imprint of HarperCollins*Publishers*,
77–85 Fulham Palace Road,
Hammersmith, London W6 8JB

Published by Fontana 1992

2 4 6 8 9 7 5 3 1

First published by
HarperCollins*Publishers* 1992

ISBN 0 00 637925 7

Photoset in Frutiger by
Rowland Phototypesetting Ltd
Bury St Edmunds, Suffolk
Printed in Great Britain by
HarperCollinsManufacturing Glasgow

CONTENTS

INTRODUCTION

When I was first asked to contribute the Foreword to this excellent publication, I was at once both exhilarated by the challenge and daunted by thoughts of the struggles to come.

How could a simple scribe such as I possibly make any worthwhile contribution to a work already o'er brimming with wit, intellectual insight and life experience? Surely any addition would be as redundant as an eighth Pillar of Wisdom or, indeed, an Eleventh Commandment. Hence I have chosen merely to document the birth of a phenomenon rather than attempt any addition to it.

On the 31st January 1984 two unknown characters played by Mel Smith and Griff Rhys Jones leant conspiratorially towards one another across an unknown table in an unknown location. They spoke for only 41 seconds but it was 41 seconds that influenced a generation. Within days youngsters of all ages had adopted the hangdog expressions, the slumped posture and above all the distinctive vocal mannerisms of the pair. Public houses, gentlemen's clubs, sports changing rooms and homes from the most exalted to the most humble echoed to the occupants' attempts to mimic the new heroes. If imitation is the sincerest form of flattery, this newly spawned pairing must have been flattered indeed.

And why not? If experience enriches our lives, these must be amongst the wealthiest men on earth. Love, marriage, divorce and death visit them on an almost daily basis. Neither are they strangers to illness, depression or debt. They suffer and in their suffering lighten the burden for the rest of us.

I trust that in this a record of some of their more poignant conversations, we can all find a spark of wit, trace of wisdom and, above all, a great deal of humour. I commend this collection to you.

Charles Hawksworth
Executive in Charge of Post Production (Carpets)
TalkBack Productions

HEADᴛᴏHEAD – THE FACTS

Who writes them?

No one. Many years ago a shepherd boy, guarding his tinder-dry flock against the incendiary intentions of French farmers, casually tossed a half-finished can of Welsh Brewers lager into the dark recesses of a nearby cave. Investigating the sound of splintering pottery which then issued forth he discovered a cache of ancient writings sealed in earthenware pots. Next to these was a cache of not-so-ancient writings in a Sainsburys bag. Thus the Head to Heads were discovered.

How are they recorded?

It is a little known fact that Mel Smith and Griff Rhys Jones have never met. They record their parts separately, Griff in the multi-million pound studio of his country retreat (also known as Lichtenstein) and Mel at the location of whichever commercial he is directing at the time. Their performances are then meshed together using satellite technology, state-of-the-art editing techniques and a team of small boys with sticky tape.

How do they remember it all?

Both Mel and Griff have prodigious memories. To demonstrate this, Mel has been known to recite the entire London business telephone directory excluding only the numbers of the more dubious mini-cab firms. This stupendous feat of recall took some eighteen hours and was, alas, the last after-dinner speech he was ever invited to make.

Do they rehearse a lot?

Fanatically. Griff has been known to phone Mel at four in the morning to run through the delivery of a certain phrase. Luckily, Mel is never in that early.

How many have they done?

There are known to be 666 Head to Head scripts in existence, a number of great significance. Theoretical physicists have calculated that it is actually impossible for this number to be exceeded without endangering the space/time continuum and the structure of matter as we know it.

Do the characters have names?
Probably.

Well, what are they?
No one knows.

What do they do for a living?
Are you a copper or something?

No, but are the characters based on anyone in particular?
Like all highly skilled character actors, Mel Smith and Griff Rhys Jones spend many painstaking hours researching the background, the speech patterns, the very essence of the characters they are about to portray. So seriously do they take this phase of preparation that they have both, time and time again, pummelled themselves with gruelling research trips to the south of France, California and several exclusive European ski resorts.

While this exhausting and exhaustive process stops short of actually visiting Peckham itself, both Mel and Griff feel that these many hours of sacrifice are worth while and that to actually visit the legendary south London borough itself or, indeed, talk to anyone who has ever been there might pitch their delicately poised performances into the realms of caricature. So, no, they're not.

FILIPINO WIVES

MEL   If something was to happen to your wife, would you get married again?

GRIFF   No, I don't think I could replace her after twenty years. She's been like a brother to me.

MEL   Of course she has.

GRIFF   And besides, I've hated every minute of it.

MEL   Really?

GRIFF   When I think back . . . the nagging, the tears, the silly tantrums. Why I do it all I don't know, but I wouldn't want to do all that to somebody else.

MEL   Yeah, only I am thinking of getting married again.

GRIFF   Again? But you've only just got divorced from Sharon.

MEL   Yeah. I don't know why I married her. Ghastly woman from a dreadful family.

GRIFF   I wouldn't say that.

MEL   Of course you wouldn't; she's your sister. Oh, no offence, mate.

GRIFF   No, of course not. But why are you so keen to get married again?

MEL   Well, apparently two out of three marriages these days ends in failure . . .

GRIFF   Exactly.

MEL   Well, I've been divorced twice, haven't I? So I reckon my next marriage is statistically bound to work.

GRIFF   Yeah, but who are you going to marry?

MEL   Well, I'm not quite sure yet. The thing is . . . I've seen this advert for Filipino wives in the back of a magazine, and I've sent off for one.

GRIFF You haven't. That's disgusting. Which magazine was this?

MEL It's not disgusting.

GRIFF You can't just see an advert and write off for a wife just like that.

MEL No, it's not just like that. Obviously you have to pay something.

GRIFF Pay?

MEL Yeah, why not? I can afford it. Some of these girls can be bought for a couple of goats.

GRIFF But you haven't got a couple of goats.

MEL They don't know that, do they?

GRIFF Well, it still sounds like prostitution to me.

MEL It's nothing like prostitution. Prostitution involves handing over large amounts of cash for sex. This Filipino wives racket costs next to nothing.

GRIFF But it's not fair on the girls.

MEL Of course it's fair on the girls. The point is, in the Philippines they live in grinding poverty and squalor – without proper housing, nutrition or health care.

GRIFF So they would feel at home in Peckham?

MEL Yeah. No, look, they're happy to come to England and marry anyone who is prepared to give them a decent roof over their head.

GRIFF You're getting your roof fixed as well, are you?

MEL Most probably, yes.

GRIFF Well, how do you know when you've selected your Miss Right . . .

MEL Miss Wong, actually.

GRIFF Miss Wong . . . how do you know you're going to love her, or even fancy her?

MEL Well, it's very straightforward. First of all I've selected her from her photograph.

GRIFF She's nice, is she?

MEL She is a stunner. I tell you what she looks like . . . what's that airline that advertises on the telly, with the gorgeous Filipino air hostesses? You know, 'Filipino girl, what a great way to fly . . . La, la, la, Filipino girl'.

GRIFF British Midland?

MEL That's the one. She looks just like one of their air hostesses.

GRIFF I see. And does she know what you look like?

MEL Well, obviously I have to send off a photograph of myself as well.

GRIFF And she fancies you?

MEL Yeah.

GRIFF . . . Was it a particularly good photograph of you?

MEL Well, actually I clipped a picture of Robert Redford out the paper. But it gives her the general idea.

GRIFF And is that all you know about each other . . . ? You know what she looks like, and she knows what Robert Redford looks like.

MEL Oh no, there's a whole dossier you get sent.

GRIFF Well, how old is she?

MEL Twenty-eight, I think. Or that could be her shoe size. They're difficult to read, some of these forms, aren't they?

GRIFF And you reckon she is the perfect woman for you?

MEL Yeah, I do, as it happens. It may seem a bit clinical, but it's like computer dating. You can cut out the distractions and get a match which you might happen upon by chance.

GRIFF So, you're definitely marrying Miss Wong.

MEL Well, it's not definite. You have to tick two other choices in case of unavailability.

GRIFF Can you send her back if she doesn't fit?

MEL Don't be ridiculous. Of course she'll fit.

GRIFF   Well, it doesn't seem quite right to me to get a wife by mail order.

MEL   Well, it's just like an arranged marriage. It's quite common practice all over the East.

GRIFF   Is it?

MEL   Oh yeah. I mean, you only have to talk to Ravi at the video shop. He wasn't allowed to marry just any girl he fancied.

GRIFF   No, of course not. He fancied Kylie Minogue.

MEL   No, his marriage was arranged for him. His family selected a suitable girl from his home village in India.

GRIFF   Right.

MEL   And one day he nips along to Heathrow airport, meets this girl he's never met before, and takes her back to his place and just gets on with it. Rather romantic, if you think about it. Knocking off a girl the first time you meet her.

GRIFF   And that was his new wife?

MEL   No, that was an air hostess he picked up outside the duty free. But in due course, his wife was delivered to him, and they have lived happily ever after.

GRIFF   Well, that's all very well for Ravi. But in your case, what about the cultural differences?

MEL   How d'you mean?

GRIFF   There would be obvious cultural differences. On the one hand, your Filipino will have her Eastern, Filipino culture. While you . . . haven't got any culture at all.

MEL   What are you talking about?

GRIFF   Well, what about food? She'll only like to eat Filipino food, whatever that is. And you like your food Indian or Chinese.

MEL   She'll get used to that . . . The point is, these girls aren't brought up like English girls. They're trained to satisfy their man's tiniest whim.

GRIFF   You mean in bed, do you?

MEL   Well, yeah.

GRIFF   And have you got a tiny whim for her to satisfy in bed?

MEL   In a way, yes. But that isn't the only side to it.

GRIFF   Exactly. She may satisfy you, you know, sexually . . . But will she bring you a cup of tea in bed? Will she make you a lovely meal of bacon and eggs and fried bread in the morning? Will she darn your socks, knit your jumpers, wash and iron a clean shirt for you every day?

MEL   Does your wife do any of that?

GRIFF   No.

MEL   Well, there you are then.

GRIFF   Is this legal?

MEL   Of course it's legal. It would only be illegal if I was bringing her over to do paid work without a permit.

GRIFF   And you're not doing that?

MEL   No, obviously, as my wife she would work for me for nothing.

NOSTALGIA

MEL I tell you one thing you notice as you get older.

GRIFF What's that, then?

MEL It's how quickly time passes. One minute you're a young man, your whole future ahead of you . . .

GRIFF Yeah.

MEL And the next minute . . .

GRIFF . . . sixty seconds has gone by.

MEL Do you realize that it's more than twenty years since 'Sergeant Pepper' came out?

GRIFF Twenty years! It's never . . .

MEL It is. It makes you think, doesn't it?

GRIFF Yeah. It makes me think, it's about time I heard it. I've always meant to.

MEL You must have heard 'Sergeant Pepper'. It's only the greatest record of all time. 'It was twenty years ago today, Sergeant Pepper taught the band to play. It's been going in and out of date. She loves you, yeah, yeah, yeah.'

GRIFF Oh yeah. Sounds brilliant.

MEL Do you know that was the first record I ever bought?

GRIFF Really?

MEL Yeah.

GRIFF Before that you used to nick them, did you?

MEL Yeah. I was a tearaway then . . . back in the sixties. It was all happening then, though, wasn't it? People these days just don't know, do they?

GRIFF They don't know. They don't know. Some of them don't know they was born.

MEL Some of them wasn't born, but what a time to be young. I mean, obviously there are some fairly good rock groups around now, and I dare say the kids of today go for today's music . . . but has there been any song in the 1970s or 1980s that can possibly compare to one of the all time greats like 'Chirpy Chirpy Cheep Cheep'?

GRIFF No. I don't think there has. There wasn't much to compare to it then.

MEL They were great days then, weren't they? Swinging London, they called it.

GRIFF Oh yeah. Where was that, then?

MEL London. Good old London town was suddenly the centre of the world for music, fashion, for youth culture. From the King's Road, Chelsea to . . . Carnaby Street just off Oxford Street. London was the place to be. Fantastic.

GRIFF Where were you living then?

MEL Devon.

GRIFF Oh, right.

MEL One great love-in, the sixties, don't you reckon?

GRIFF Yeah. It was for me.

MEL Yeah?

GRIFF Yeah, I had one love-in round the back of the bus shelter in 1967. I didn't get my next until about 1979.

MEL Of course I was very much involved with hippie culture. You know, West Coast.

GRIFF Yeah, well, you would be in Devon.

MEL I mean, West Coast of America. San Francisco, Los Angeles . . . New York. I was one of the beautiful people.

GRIFF   That is a surprise. I don't remember that.

MEL   Well, it was probably before I met you.

GRIFF   Well, it must be, because you've always been as ugly as sin since I've known you.

MEL   Who was that rockstar who got so drugged up and choked on his own vomit?

GRIFF   Jim Morrison?

MEL   No, not him, the other one.

GRIFF   Keith Moon? Mama Cass? Janis Joplin? Frank Ifield?

MEL   No.

GRIFF   Jimi Hendrix?

MEL   That's the one.

GRIFF   Oh, right! What about him?

MEL   Well, he died. Choked to death on his own vomit.

GRIFF   Did he really? Well, who'd've thought it?

MEL   Yeah, now he did have some marvellous records.

GRIFF   Yeah. He used to do that great tune: 'Ooh ooh oh ooh . . . '

MEL   No, no, no. It went, 'Oooooh Oooooh Ohohooooh.'

GRIFF   No, that's stupid, that's Jimmy Page. Jimi Hendrix was, 'Oooh oooh oooh.'

MEL   Unforgettable stuff.

GRIFF   Fantastic tune. Who wrote it?

MEL   Lionel Bart. It was a great tune, wasn't it? Do you remember all those Bank Holiday fights at Southend and Brighton? Mods v Rockers.

GRIFF   You don't have to ask me if I remember that.

MEL   Well, do you?

GRIFF   Yes. I was right in the middle, I was right in the thick of it, I was.

MEL   You were there?

GRIFF   I was there on the beach with the best of them.

MEL Which were you, then? A Mod or a Rocker?

GRIFF Neither, I was the deck-chair attendant. It was murder, chasing those Rods and Mockers, and they never paid for the chairs neither.

MEL I was a Mod I was.

GRIFF No, never.

MEL I was.

GRIFF Well, you're more of a skinhead now, aren't you?

MEL Yeah, all right. But it was very tribal then. I mean, I was a Mod. What were you?

GRIFF I don't know.

MEL What gear did you go around in then? What did you look like?

GRIFF Well, I had long hair.

MEL Did you have sideboards?

GRIFF No. Well, we had a cupboard at home for the drinks at Christmas.

MEL What did you wear?

GRIFF I used to have pink flowery shirts.

MEL With big collars?

GRIFF Oh yeah, with the big nine-inch collars.

MEL Yeah.

GRIFF A kipper tie, eight inches wide.

MEL Flared trousers?

GRIFF To a certain extent. In about 1969 I got into these crushed velvet loons, about twenty-five inches round the ankles.

MEL A bit like the ones you had on the other night.

GRIFF Yeah, they *were* the ones I had on the other night. And of course I had six-inch platform soles and an Afghan jacket, beads and a tattoo on my arm saying 'I love Simon Dee'.

MEL   I get the picture.

GRIFF   What do you reckon that made me?

MEL   That's easy. You were a prat.

MILLIONAIRES

MEL I've had a bit of luck.

GRIFF What's that, then?

MEL I'll give you a clue. 'Money makes the world go round, the world go round, the world go round . . . ' 'Money, money, money, It's a rich man's world . . . ' 'If I was a rich man, diddle liddle, liddle, diddle . . . ' What do you think I've won, then?

GRIFF Singing lessons?

MEL No. I've had a win come up on the pools.

GRIFF Yeah? How much?

MEL Five, zero, zero, zero.

GRIFF What? Five thousand pounds?

MEL Fifty point nought nought pence.

GRIFF That's not much.

MEL Yeah, well, I'm in a syndicate at work. Altogether we won a hundred thousand pounds, but there's two hundred thousand in the syndicate, you see. Still, it's a start. You know what they say . . . From little acorns do great sycamores grow . . .

GRIFF You going to buy some acorns, then?

MEL Eh? No, it's a figure of speech. I'm going to invest it. I'm going to put my fifty pence into something.

GRIFF What, like a cigarette machine?

MEL No, I'm talking about stocks and shares, or better still, the property market. I'm going to put my money in bricks and mortar.

GRIFF How many bricks are you going to get for fifty pee?

MEL Well . . .

GRIFF You get 'bout a half brick for that.

MEL It's a start.

GRIFF Yeah, you could lob it through a jeweller's window, grab yourself a fortune.

MEL You may mock, but all these millionaires started with nothing.

GRIFF Oh, well, *you're* well away then, aren't you?

MEL I mean, look at that Robert Maxwell. When he came over here from . . . abroad . . . he didn't have two ha'pennies to spend together. But now he's filthy rich, isn't he? He can cock his snook at anyone. Last year, he bought the *Daily Mirror*.

GRIFF Well, that's nothing. I bought a *Daily Mirror* this morning.

MEL No, he bought the whole thing, the building, the printing works, the workers, everything you get with a newspaper.

GRIFF The bingo cards?

MEL Probably. But the whole thing is his property, his plaything.

GRIFF So he could make them put his picture on the front page and have all the stories written about himself.

MEL Yeah, he could in theory, yes. Why?

GRIFF Because that's what the *Mirror* was like this morning.

MEL Well, that shows you what it means to be a millionaire.

GRIFF Yeah, not minding how many readers your newspapers lose.

MEL Of course, he isn't the richest man in the country.

GRIFF Oh no, who is then? Paul McCartney, John Paul Getty?

MEL Richard Stilgoe.

GRIFF Richard Stilgoe. No . . .

MEL He's the richest man going.

GRIFF How's that, then?

MEL   Well, for a start off, he gets a million quid a day off that *Starlight Express*.

GRIFF   Does he? What is *Starlight Express*? Is it like a credit card?

MEL   No!

GRIFF   It's a newspaper, is it?

MEL   No, it's a show of some sort. It's been running up the West End for ages. And he's got another one on the go, *Phantom of the Opera*, another million out of that. And the BBC still owe him some money for being on Esther Rantzen's programme a couple of years back, and he's still doing 'Start the Week'.

GRIFF   He's the same painful little jerk he ever was, is he? Only richer.

MEL   Yeah. Now the only ones richer than him is whatsisnames, the Windsors.

GRIFF   You mean . . .

MEL   Yeah.

GRIFF   What, Barbara Windsor and that husband of hers that had that trouble.

MEL   No, I mean *the* Windsors. The Royals. They own . . . well, they own everything in the country, don't they?

GRIFF   Yeah, I suppose they do.

MEL   They own Cornwall. Wales. And England. They own all of England. And Scotland, of course.

GRIFF   The Queen Mother brought that with her, didn't she?

MEL   Yeah.

GRIFF   And Northern Ireland, they own that.

MEL   As a tax dodge, yes.

GRIFF   It must be great being rich, eh?

MEL   It's fan-bloody-tastic, I can tell you.

GRIFF   Yeah. Well, you can't tell me because you're not rich, are you?

MEL   No.

GRIFF And you never have been.

MEL Not really, no. Look, what would you do if you got a million pounds then, eh? It's difficult, isn't it?

GRIFF Well, I'd definitely buy a new swing-top bin for the kitchen, 'cos that pedal one is useless.

MEL Look, a million pounds must make more difference to you than just a swing-top dustbin.

GRIFF Oh yeah. Well, I wouldn't have to get up and go to work every morning.

MEL Well, you don't now. You've been unemployed for over two years, what are you talking about?

GRIFF Well, I wouldn't have to tramp down the dole office every Thursday any more.

MEL No, I suppose you wouldn't.

GRIFF No, I could buy myself a Rolls Royce and drive down instead.

MEL What you've got to remember is that money can't buy you everything.

GRIFF No . . . can't it? What can't it buy?

MEL Happiness, my friend, happiness. Do you think that just because you've got untold wealth you'll be blissfully happy?

GRIFF Well, it had crossed my mind, yeah.

MEL No, no. Money has its problems too. Think about the women.

GRIFF Well, they're no problem when you're rich, are they?

MEL Of course they are. You suddenly got a load of money, the women will be like flies round a honey pot, mate.

GRIFF Will they?

MEL Oh yeah. All those model girls, beautiful jet setters, the Jerry Halls and all that. One sniff of your filthy lucre and they'll suck you dry.

GRIFF Will they really?

MEL Oh yeah, definitely.

GRIFF You wouldn't want all them women after you, if you had all the money, then?

MEL No. If I was rich I wouldn't go with any old beautiful woman who was just after my money. They'd have to be interested in my personality, my brains, my body.

GRIFF And if they didn't go for all that?

MEL Then I'd offer them some money.

GRIFF Oh yeah.

MEL You see, it's all right having the money. Hanging on to it is the difficult bit. I mean, look at that Paul Getty. The Mafia kidnapped his grandson and demanded a huge ransom.

GRIFF Right.

MEL And a week later they send him one of the kid's ears through the post.

GRIFF What, in an envelope, like?

MEL Yeah, I suppose so. Or a jiffy bag or something.

GRIFF Or Earmail.

MEL Yeah. It doesn't matter how they sent the bleeding ear.

GRIFF But what did they do it for then? Cut off his ear and send it like that?

MEL To prove they really had got his grandson.

GRIFF Well, how did Paul Getty know it was his grandson's ear? They could have just sent one of their own ears.

MEL No, he'd recognize it. You'd recognize your own grandson's ear, wouldn't you?

GRIFF No, I wouldn't.

MEL Why not?

GRIFF I haven't got a grandson.

MEL Well, Paul Getty did recognize his grandson's ear.

GRIFF Perhaps it still had his cigar stuck behind it.

MEL Probably. And the demand came with it: pay up or else.

GRIFF Or else what?

MEL Or else they'd cut off another prominent bit of his body and send that.

GRIFF He shouldn't have paid up, should he?

MEL Why not?

GRIFF Well, eventually he'd have got his grandson back, bit by bit, if he'd hung on, like in instalments. A millionaire and you've got a grandson like a Meccano set. Well, what would you do with a million pounds?

MEL I'd probably travel the world and see all the sights I'd never seen but always talked about seeing.

GRIFF Do you think Joanna Lumley would let you, then?

MEL No, I was talking about the ancient ruins.

GRIFF So was I.

MEL Oh no, no. I'd be generous. For example, to each of my friends I would give . . . a thousand pounds.

GRIFF Oh, I see. So what would you do with the other 999,000 pounds, then?

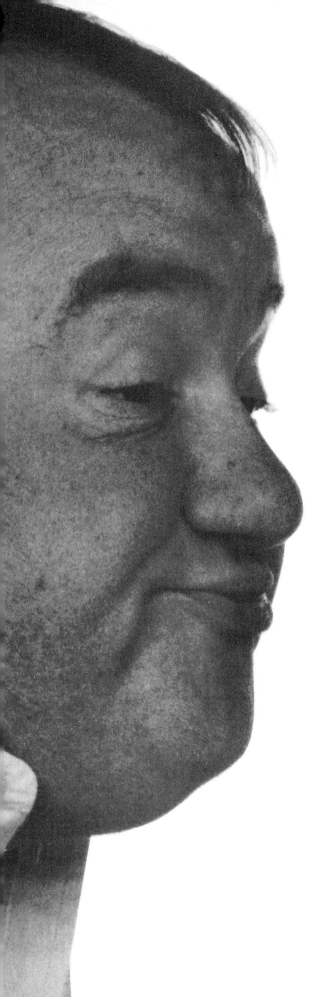

FASHION

MEL I'm thinking of having my ears pierced.

GRIFF What, have they got wax in them, have they?

MEL Eh?

GRIFF I said, HAVE THEY GOT WAX IN THEM?

MEL No, having them pierced, not syringed.

GRIFF Oh. Why?

MEL To put an earring in. Very fashionable, mate. All the rage.

GRIFF Only with poofters and pirates.

MEL No, no. Fashion's the in thing, isn't it. It's important, because your appearance, your clothes make a statement about you, they say something.

GRIFF Like yours are saying, 'I'm a scruffy bastard'.

MEL No, that's just where you are wrong. Look, you're completely ignorant about this sort of thing, aren't you?

GRIFF No, I'm not ignorant. I just don't know anything about it.

MEL That's it, you see, there's always been the fashion leaders down the ages: Beau Brummel, Beau Nash . . .

GRIFF Bo Derek.

MEL Bo Derek, yeah, him as well.

GRIFF Bo Diddley . . .

MEL Yeah.

GRIFF Bo Beep . . .

MEL Yeah, well, it's the same today, isn't it? What Princess Di wears today, the girl in the street wears tomorrow.

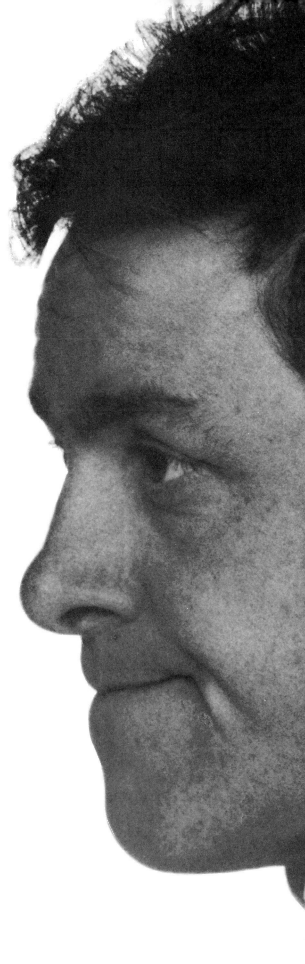

GRIFF Right. She only wears things once, then gives them to some girl in the street. That's generous, isn't it?

MEL No, look, she sets the style for the women of Britain. She's a fashion leader. Those of us in the know, like, we *know* what's fashionable. We're fashion conscious, not like you. You're obviously fashion unconscious, fashion sleep-walking, you are.

GRIFF Well, how do you know what's fashionable, then?

MEL Well, I read the papers.

GRIFF I didn't know they had a fashion page in the *Sporting Life*.

MEL And I keep my eyes open. If I'm in some trendy eating place and Bryan Ferry walks in or Sebastian Coe, I can see what . . .

GRIFF They're regulars down the Deptford Spud-U-Like, are they?

MEL I can see what they're wearing, and they can see what I'm wearing.

GRIFF Well, what are you wearing? You don't dress up in like evening jackets or nothing.

MEL No, I dress in what we call smart casual.

GRIFF What's that, then?

MEL Well, you've seen on the television, England footballers like Glenn Hoddle or Kevin Keegan. You've seen how they dress. I'm a bit like them.

GRIFF You mean, you wear a white shirt and blue shorts.

MEL Not like when they're on the field. When they're being interviewed afterwards or on 'Question of Sport' or something. Look, see this shirt?

GRIFF Yes.

MEL This is a high-quality shirt. You wouldn't believe what I paid for this shirt.

GRIFF Fifty pence?

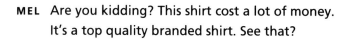

MEL   Are you kidding? This shirt cost a lot of money. It's a top quality branded shirt. See that?

GRIFF   What, your tit?

MEL   No, little alligator.

GRIFF   It's an alligator shirt, is it?

MEL   No, they are called Lacoste.

GRIFF   Not alligator.

MEL   No, Lacoste. It's French for alligator, isn't it?

GRIFF   I see.

MEL   The interesting thing is that the colour of that alligator changes every year.

GRIFF   Does it?

MEL   Yep.

GRIFF   Well, that's what I call really smart. I hope you wear that shirt New Year's Eve, I'll watch it change colour . . .

MEL   Eh? No . . .

GRIFF   It's more like a chameleon.

MEL   It doesn't work like that. This one here doesn't actually change. They change the colour at the factory every year.

GRIFF   So you send your shirt back for a colour change?

MEL   No, of course not. You buy a new shirt.

GRIFF   Every year?

MEL   Yeah.

GRIFF   Blimey.

MEL   I mean, how do you select your clothes?

GRIFF   Obviously I take a great interest. If my wife buys something and I don't like it, I tell her.

MEL   Your wife?

GRIFF   She knows about fashion. She gets all them glossy fashion magazines like . . .

MEL   *Vogue* and *Harpers*?

GRIFF   Littlewoods and the Freeman catalogue, because
        that Lulu knows a thing or two. She's one of
        them fashion leaders you was talking about.

MEL   Oh yeah, very street cred, Lulu.

GRIFF   No, like you say. What Lulu wears today . . .

MEL   . . . Lulu is still wearing tomorrow. Look, how do
        you decide what to put on in the morning? Do
        you use your eyesight at all?

GRIFF   No, I go more by sense of smell. Whichever pair of
        socks that seems freshest, I bung them on.

MEL   Well, I reckon you should get yourself a whole
        new wardrobe.

GRIFF   No, I've got a wardrobe. Half the time I haven't
        got enough clothes to go in it.

MEL   It's the clothes I'm talking about. Treat yourself to
        a nice Italian suit.

GRIFF   Oh yeah, Italian.

MEL   Mohair's nice.

GRIFF   Right. What exactly is a Mo?

MEL   What?

GRIFF   Sheepskin jacket, right, that comes from a sheep
        or fox fur, that's a fox's fur.

MEL   A fox's fur, that's right.

GRIFF   Well, what's a Mo, then, that they get the Mo-
        hair from?

MEL   Well, it's a special sort of animal. You see them
        running around in Italy.

GRIFF   What's it like, then?

MEL   Well, it's got this lovely good quality hair or fur, a
        bit shiny it is and soft, like an Italian suit in fact.

GRIFF   But without the buttons.

MEL   Obviously without the buttons. They put the
        buttons on later.

GRIFF   I just bought a new jacket.

MEL   What animal is that from?

GRIFF   Donkey.

MEL   Yeah, you see, you've got to work to make yourself fashionable and famous.

GRIFF   Oh, right.

MEL   Because fame can be prone to the fickle hand of fashion like anything else. Take Simon Dee.

GRIFF   Who?

MEL   Exactly. One minute he's the highest paid man in Britain, next minute, bang . . . he's got his own series on the BBC.

GRIFF   Tragic.

MEL   He was never heard of again. That's showbiz. Lady Fame is a fickle girl . . .

GRIFF   Yeah.

MEL   Lady Fame, here today, gone tomorrow.

GRIFF   Yeah.

MEL   The fickle Lady Fame.

GRIFF   Yeah. I never liked her husband either.

MEL   Eh?

GRIFF   That singer bloke, Georgie. Terrible . . . 'I say yeah, yeah . . . That's what I say, I say yeah, yeah . . .'

MEL   Yeah, all right.

GRIFF   Awful. So . . . that's why you're getting your ears pierced, then, so you'll end up like Georgie Fame or Simon Dee?

MEL   Something like that.

GRIFF   Then all over the country all the kids will be trying to look like you.

MEL   Yes, that's quite possible.

GRIFF   Blimey, a whole generation of fat bald teenagers.

DIETS

GRIFF I ain't half hungry. My missus has put me on a diet.

MEL Did she?

GRIFF Yes. She's got this book: she put me on the Beverley Hills H-Bomb diet and every day I have to eat a specific amount of things.

MEL What, tiny amounts?

GRIFF Oh, yes. Tiny. This is my fifth day.

MEL What have you got to eat today, then?

GRIFF I don't know. I ate the book I was so hungry. She'll be furious, my missus, when she finds out.

MEL Oh, I shouldn't worry about it.

GRIFF Why's that, then?

MEL 'Cos dieting makes you fat.

GRIFF Well, you must have been on a lot of diets, then. To get the size you are.

MEL No, no, no. I'm not fat, just big boned. You're fat.

GRIFF Don't you think that if you didn't drink fourteen pints and eat two curries every night your bones might be smaller?

MEL No, it's irrelevant. I had a friend who went on one of them high-fibre diets.

GRIFF What's that, then?

MEL Well, it's basically bran. You can eat what you like but you've got to have some bran on it. So you have a bowl of cornflakes and a little bit of bran on top. Egg, bacon, tomato, sausage, fried bread, black pudding and a little bit of bran on top.

GRIFF Cup of tea?

MEL Yes, and a little bit of bran on top.

GRIFF McDonalds?

MEL   Yes, bran.

GRIFF   Pint of beer?

MEL   Bran.

GRIFF   Don't that make the beer taste a bit funny?

MEL   You don't really notice after the eighteenth pint.

GRIFF   You mean, your friend doesn't notice?

MEL   What?

GRIFF   Your friend what's on the diet.

MEL   Oh yes, yes.

GRIFF   All this bran, doesn't it make you want to go to the . . .

MEL   What?

GRIFF   You know. Want to go to the . . .

MEL   Oh, to the bran shop to get some more bran. Yes, it does.

GRIFF   No, the boghouse, the carsey.

MEL   Oh, the toilet. Yes, you're never off it. Well, that's how the diet works. You spend so much time in the lavatory that you haven't got time to go out and buy any proper food. I mean, it's straight down the supermarket and up to the checkout with an empty cardboard box and a trolley.

GRIFF   How long do you do this bran diet for?

MEL   What, my friend?

GRIFF   Oh, yes, your friend.

MEL   For about four days.

GRIFF   It's bad to go on longer, is it?

MEL   Ooh, terrible. You run out of bog paper. I mean, it gets desperate. You try kitchen paper, unravelling the cardboard bit in the middle of the bog roll. It's just no good.

GRIFF   So your friend, he didn't lose any weight, then?

MEL   He lost four stone, ate one chocolate biscuit and put it all back on again.

GRIFF   That's sad.

MEL   Well, I think it's nature. It's your metabolisms.

GRIFF   What's that, then?

MEL   Well, basically, if you've got a problem with your metabolisms then you're buggered.

GRIFF   Why don't you stop eating them, then? Why don't you say to your wife, 'I don't want to eat any more of these metabolisms,' and put them on the side of the plate?

MEL   No, you don't understand. You don't eat metabolisms. You've got them inside of you.

GRIFF   What, like piles?

MEL   Yes, and you've got them for life.

GRIFF   Don't you think, if you don't diet, that you should do that exercise thing?

MEL   No, no, exercise makes you fat.

GRIFF   Well, what about that Jane Fonda?

MEL   Enormous. Obese.

GRIFF   But I've seen her on TV with all those girls in leotards wiggling about doing that aerotic dancing thing.

MEL   No, it's all trick photography, done with mirrors. I mean, take Twiggy, she should be called Trunky – one pile of flab.

GRIFF   So dieting and exercise doesn't do you any good?

MEL   I would have to run a mile to get rid of what calories I get out of every pint of beer that I bought.

GRIFF   Well, that's all right then. I mean, you usually run a mile before you buy a pint of beer, don't you?

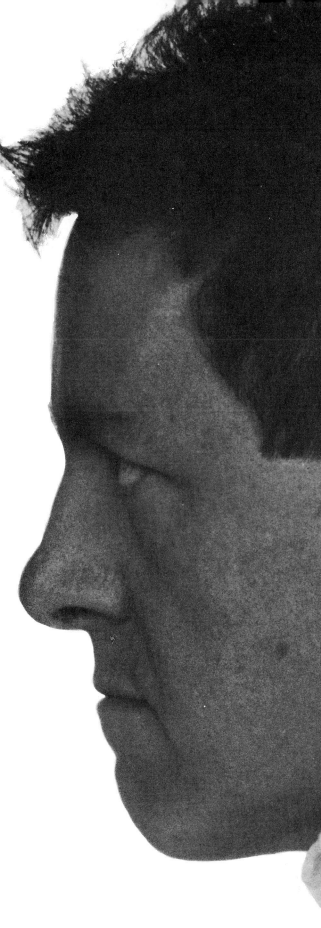

SPERM BANK

MEL   I went down to Harley Street yesterday. You know, where the clinics are and all that.

GRIFF   Oh yeah?

MEL   I go down there quite often to the artificial inseminatory, the sperm bank, you know. 'Cos they got the biggest collection of sperms in the country.

GRIFF   What, you go down there and have a look at them, do you?

MEL   No, I go to stick some in. I'm a donator.

GRIFF   How d'you do that, then?

MEL   What?

GRIFF   I mean, how come? No, I mean how does it come about that you go down there, then?

MEL   Well, there's a lot of women in the world and a lot of them, for various reasons, can't get pregnant . . . 'cos their husbands haven't got it in them.

GRIFF   Not at all?

MEL   Not as much as I have. And obviously they need a virile manly sperm to be stuck in there and do the business. I'm not being too technical, am I?

GRIFF   How many of these women are there, then?

MEL   Hundreds.

GRIFF   You're more virile than I thought you were. When you go down there do they give you a choice of women?

MEL   No, I don't see the women.

GRIFF   So it's like at home, then.

MEL   Eh?

GRIFF   Well, it's in the dark with the light out.

MEL   No. She's not actually there.

GRIFF   Where is she?

MEL   Well, I don't know. Out shopping or something. She's not actually expecting it there and then.

GRIFF   Just like home, isn't it?

MEL   It's like a bank. It's a sperm bank. I go down and leave a little deposit and she goes down later and makes a withdrawal, just like a bank.

GRIFF   I expect there's a bit of a queue there on Fridays.

MEL   Undoubtedly.

GRIFF   So when you go down there, what happens?

MEL   There's no fuss, it's like donating blood – one little prick and it's over. You really don't notice it at all.

GRIFF   You wouldn't, would you? So do they give you a hand?

MEL   What?

GRIFF   Do they give you any help?

MEL   Yes. Well, a nurse does.

GRIFF   How does a nurse help you, then?

MEL   Well, she gives you the bottle.

GRIFF   What, like a milk bottle?

MEL   Sort of.

GRIFF   That's nearly a pint!

MEL   Yes, but you aren't expected to fill it.

GRIFF   Just half full or whatever.

MEL   Yes, or whatever. You work at your own pace.

GRIFF   It's like a business, ain't it? Do they give you money?

MEL   Obviously they do pay you. But I don't do it for the money. I get a lot of personal satisfaction out of it.

TELEPATHY

MEL I want to try a little experiment.

GRIFF Right, yes.

MEL OK. I want you to think of a simple shape, OK? And then I'm going to try and work out what it is that you're thinking of by picking up on the electrical impulses coming off your brain.

GRIFF What, like a simple shape, like a square or something like that?

MEL Yeah. Well, yeah it could have been a square, but you've said that now.

GRIFF Oh yeah, right. You mean a simple shape?

MEL Right.

GRIFF Like a circle or a triangle or a square?

MEL Yeah, well, I mean it could have been a circle or a triangle or a square, but not now. Obviously it wants to be a different shape . . .

GRIFF Something else?

MEL Yeah, that's right. OK.

GRIFF What is the difference between an oblong and a rectangle?

MEL Get on with it!

GRIFF Oh, sorry, yeah. Hang on . . . I've got it now, I've got it . . .

MEL You've got it, you've got it . . . Is it a dodecahedron?

GRIFF Hold on a minute, hold on a minute, hold on . . . No.

MEL Well, what is it, then?

GRIFF It's a hat.

MEL A hat?

GRIFF A hat, yes.

MEL No, look. There is a way of making this work. I tell you what, OK? Now look, just think of anything you like. Anything. Don't matter what . . .

GRIFF Anything?

MEL Anything, OK? And then try and transfer those thoughts into my brain. Now try. Work hard at it . . .

GRIFF I can't think of anything.

MEL Oh, for Heaven's sake!

GRIFF Well, hang on, hang on . . . I've got something now. Hurry up 'cos I can't keep it all day.

MEL Right, right . . . Is it a tent?

GRIFF No.

MEL Is it a balloon?

GRIFF No.

MEL Is it a whale?

GRIFF No.

MEL What is it?

GRIFF It's Elizabeth Taylor. You see, you're a million miles away. Although actually, funnily enough . . .

MEL Well, of course, I'm a member of MENSA.

GRIFF You never are!

MEL Yes, I am.

GRIFF What? That old organization for, like, the intelligent and the brainy people? You never are!

MEL I am.

GRIFF Well, they can't be that intelligent if they let you in.

MEL Well, no, I had to prove myself, mate.

GRIFF Oh, did you?

MEL Oh yeah. I saw this advertisement in a magazine and they had this very difficult problem that you had to solve.

GRIFF Oh really?

MEL Oh yeah.

GRIFF   Where was this?

MEL   This was in the back of the *Reader's Digest*.

GRIFF   Oh, right, yeah. And when was this?

MEL   Oh about, what, two years ago. Anyway, last week I finished it and I posted it to them with a cheque for four hundred quid and then they sent back my membership.

GRIFF   Oh yeah, four hundred quid? Well, they're not stupid, then, at MENSA, are they?

MEL   No, they're not. That's what I'm saying. They've very high IQs.

GRIFF   Have they?

MEL   Very high IQs.

GRIFF   But, I mean, you haven't got a high IQ.

MEL   A high IQ?

GRIFF   A high I, IQ . . .

MEL   My IQ is huge!

GRIFF   Is it?

MEL   I went in with an IQ of 150.

GRIFF   You're kidding!

MEL   After two meetings there it was up to 175.

GRIFF   My God!

MEL   Yeah. Then I watched a couple of television programmes with Noel Edmonds in and it went back down to 96.

HUMOUR

GRIFF I tell you someone I do find funny . . .

MEL Who's that?

GRIFF Noel Edwards. He is a serious comic genius.

MEL Do you really think so?

GRIFF No, I don't, not at all, but those phone calls, those phone calls. Hah hah. He just picks up that phone, doesn't he, he doesn't care. He just phones somebody and he pretends to be somebody, right, but he's not really them. He's just pretending. He doesn't care. Yeah. Maybe it would be like a policeman ringing up to tell them that their wife has been knocked over in an accident and is dead, right, and they all get all windy, like, and then he leads them along a bit and says how she's got all mangled and squashed and then just when they're getting choked, he says, 'No, no, do you know who this is?' and they say, 'No,' and he says, 'It's Noel Edwards, it's Noel Edwards,' he says, and this is the bit that creases me up, they say, 'What?' and he's winding them up, see, and it's like a wind-up, like, and he says, 'What, my wife's not dead after all?' and Noel says, 'No, not so far as I know,' and the bloke right, he's confused.

MEL Well, yes, he probably would be.

GRIFF 'So my wife is alive and not dead?' he says and, as quick as anything, Noel says they're on the radio, so he says, 'Hah hah ha,' right, instead of, 'Why don't you fuck off, you mindless cunt,' and that makes me laugh. I don't know why.

MEL Well, it's your humour.

GRIFF It's my humour. Mine and Noel's. We don't care.

GRIFF What are we going to talk about now?

MEL   I don't know.

GRIFF   Do you know any jokes?

MEL   Yeah, all right, I'll tell you a joke. Stop me if you've heard it before.

GRIFF   All right.

MEL   Stop me if you've heard it.

GRIFF   Right, stop.

MEL   What?

GRIFF   I've heard it before.

MEL   How can you possibly know you've heard it?

GRIFF   The last time you told me a joke, it was the other day, you started with 'Stop me if you've heard it before.'

MEL   I haven't started yet. You can't stop me before I've started.

GRIFF   Can't I?

MEL   Listen, you'll love this. A man goes into a pub . . .

GRIFF   Oh, I have heard it.

MEL   What?

GRIFF   I've heard your joke before. I can't remember how it ends but I remember the beginning. A man goes in the pub, it was very good.

MEL   But this is a different man.

GRIFF   Well, how am I supposed to know that?

MEL   Just take it from me. It's a different man.

GRIFF   Oh, all right. I see.

MEL   Anyway, this different man goes into a pub . . .

GRIFF   Is it a different pub?

MEL   It doesn't matter. I don't know. Yes, no, this is a joke. It's just a man going into a pub.

GRIFF   He doesn't order a dog-shit sandwich, does he?

MEL   No, he doesn't. He goes into a pub.

GRIFF   Yeah. Hah-ha.

MEL   I haven't finished the joke yet.

GRIFF   Yeah, I know, but I'm laughing already because I remember how it ends.

MEL   Oh, for Heaven's sake, I'm not telling any jokes.

GRIFF   I like a good laugh.

MEL   Me too. But they can go too far, these comedians these days . . .

GRIFF   Oh yeah. On the telly the other day I saw this show, right, where these geezers was all jumping off a burning oil rig. All in flames into the water. It was too much, gone too far.

MEL   Where was this?

GRIFF   On the news.

MEL   What, on the news on television?

GRIFF   That's right. All in flames in their little yellow oil suits, wriggling around as they fell through the air. I mean, I laughed, it's my humour, but it's not right. They've gone too far.

TELEVISION

MEL I've got my satellite dish up now.

GRIFF You get good reception, do you?

MEL Oh yes, fantastic . . . I can pick up television channels from all round the world direct on my own TV set.

GRIFF BBC2?

MEL No, I can't get that, as it happens . . . Still, there's never much on that, is there?

GRIFF No.

MEL No.

GRIFF Can you get Channel 4?

MEL You know, I've never tried. I *can* get French, Italian, Russian, even Spanish.

GRIFF And are they good programmes?

MEL Christ knows, they're all in a foreign language.

GRIFF So how does this satellite TV work, then? I mean, what I don't understand is, how come out of all the millions of houses, how do they know to beam down programmes from the beaming machine to your house?

MEL What do you mean, how do they know? Don't be so naive. They see my ruddy great white dish on my roof and they go, 'There's one now. Beam it down, Scotty.'

GRIFF Which is why it's so big?

MEL Exactly. So it can be seen from outer space.

GRIFF No. There's no point in buying it now, too expensive. I'll wait three years until they come down in price.

MEL Well, if you thought like that you would never buy anything. You'd still have a black-and-white TV.

GRIFF I still have got a black-and-white TV set.

MEL You haven't!

GRIFF Well, the licence is that much cheaper.

MEL You haven't got a licence, have you?

GRIFF Well, no, of course not, but . . . You see, I don't see the point of having a colour TV, not for me, anyway. I only ever watch one thing.

MEL What's that, then?

GRIFF Snooker.

MEL Oh. I suppose you haven't got a video either.

GRIFF What's a video?

MEL A video recorder. You know, you have videos from the video shop.

GRIFF Oh yeah. And tell me, do you ever get hold of any of those ee-oo-ah videos.

MEL What, Phil Cool?

GRIFF No, you know, blue videos.

MEL I'm interested in films. Did you ever see that film *The Postman Always Knocks Her About a Bit* with Jack Nicholson and Francis de La Tour? They said that when they made that film, they actually did it.

GRIFF What, actually overacted?

MEL Yeah. Mind you, I've seen some great films, Renoir, Scorsese, Capola, but of all the films I ever seen the best one I ever saw was this woman fucking a pig.

GRIFF Oh yeah, and what was that like?

MEL It was fairly basic, of course, lot of squealing and so on. But I liked it. I was in a porn film once.

GRIFF Were you?

MEL Yeah. I had a small part.

GRIFF Oh really. I think you still have, haven't you?

MEL No, I mean, I wasn't playing a big role, in fact, most of the time I was a stand-in.

GRIFF What does that mean, then?

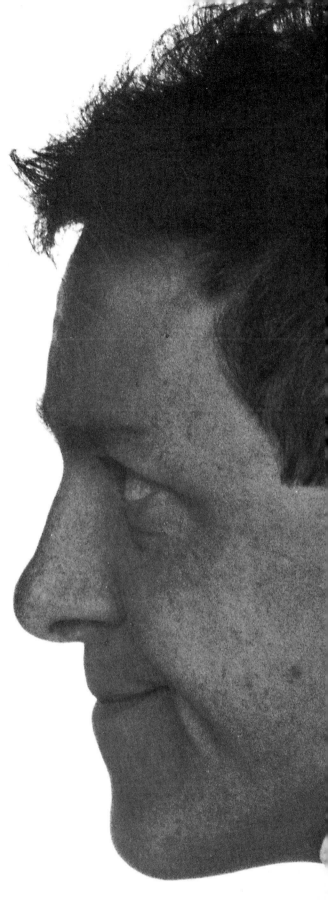

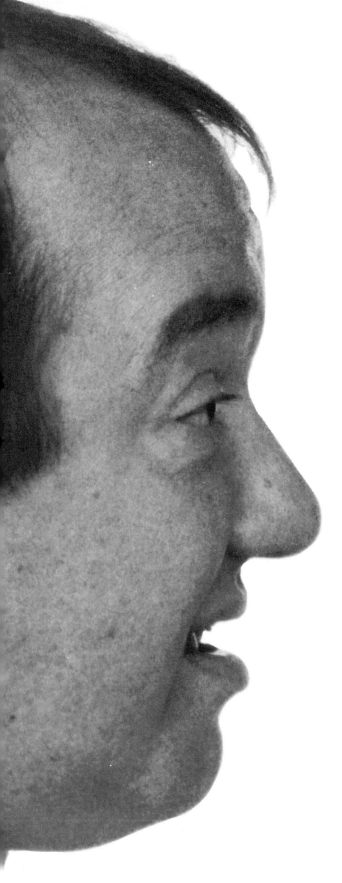

MEL Well, when they weren't shooting they got me to sort of step in. I only did it because I was a bit hard up at the time.

GRIFF Short of money?

MEL That's right, yeah.

GRIFF So, did they pay you a lot for doing it?

MEL No, but I got a lot of personal satisfaction from my work.

GRIFF What exactly did you do? Did you do a lot of things?

MEL Well, there was a little bit of French, a little bit of Italian.

GRIFF What's that, then?

MEL Fellatio.

GRIFF What's that, then, fellatio?

MEL Haven't you ever seen a blue film?

GRIFF Yeah, I saw one once.

MEL Was it hard?

GRIFF After a little bit.

MEL You know the difference between hard and soft porn films?

GRIFF No, I don't, really.

MEL Well, hard is where you can see the erect male member and soft is where it isn't. So what about this film you saw, then?

GRIFF Well, it was hard core, then it was soft core, then it was hard core again. The way I see it is, there is nothing wrong with sex films. What I can't understand is all this violence.

MEL Neither can I. I went down to Mr Patel's the other day and got a video called *The Return of the Flesh Eating Zombies* with their chain saws and axes. Do you know what?

GRIFF What?

MEL Turned out to be a video nasty. This is dreadful. They ought to put a warning on the box or something. I mean, it was awful. There were these zombies leapt on this girl in a car. They chopped her head off, threw away the brain and ate the eyeballs. Now where's the pleasure in that?

GRIFF Well, it depends on whether you like eyeballs or not, I suppose.

MEL But what interested me in a film like that is the technique. In the film, it doesn't give me the willies or anything like that. A film like that, you've got to remember that it's not a head with real brains in it . . .

GRIFF It's a model.

MEL Yeah, a model or an actress or something like that.

GRIFF Don't you think there's a link between those films and the crime rate?

MEL In what way?

GRIFF Well, people watch those films and then they go out and beat up the cinema managers. But can you remember the first time you had sex?

MEL Well, yes, I can, funnily enough.

GRIFF How's that?

MEL Well, I remember it very clearly because . . . I can remember it very clearly because President Kennedy was being assassinated on the television at the time.

NIGHTMARE

GRIFF   At the moment, I'm having this terrible recurring nightmare.

MEL   Ooh. What is it?

GRIFF   It's a dream that comes over and over again.

MEL   Yeah, I know, but what happens in it?

GRIFF   Oh, well, I'm at school, right.

MEL   Yeah.

GRIFF   And it's in the middle of the day, right.

MEL   Yeah.

GRIFF   And there I am wearing nothing but this extremely short vest and, no matter how hard I pull it, it won't sort of, like, it won't cover my . . .

MEL   It won't cover your embarrassment.

GRIFF   It won't cover my cock.

MEL   Yeah. But don't worry about that, 'cos that's really quite common.

GRIFF   Is it? Well, Marks & Spencer should do something about it.

MEL   No, not the vest, the dream. A lot of people have that dream. You see, it's apparently . . . basically you're feeling guilty about something, you see, you're feeling inadequate . . . about something.

GRIFF   Am I?

MEL   Yeah. You've got a sense of repressed guilt about something that happened to you long ago in your past. Are you feeling guilty about anything?

GRIFF   No, not really. Except that time I went to school without any trousers on. Funnily enough, I'm not sleeping at the moment. I can't sleep at all.

MEL You know what that is. Insomnia. Have you tried counting sheep?

GRIFF 'Course I have.

MEL What happened?

GRIFF Well, it was freezing. It's bloody cold out there in the middle of the field. Anyway, there were only a hundred.

MEL You're not supposed to *go* there.

GRIFF Oh.

MEL You're supposed to imagine the sheep jumping over a fence, see. One sheep, two sheep, you count them, you see? One sheep, two sheep, er, three sheep, four sheep, see? It's being monotonous, isn't it? Here, wake up!

GRIFF Sorry. Sorry, I'd nodded off there.

MEL Cor, dear! Well, that's what you want to do, isn't it, you want to count the sheep.

GRIFF Well, it'd be no good when I was trying to get to sleep.

MEL Why not?

GRIFF Well, it'd be too dark for me to see them. I might, I might ruin my eyesight.

MEL Yeah, but you don't actually see them, do you, it's in your mind's eye, the sheep. Can't you imagine it's the daytime?

GRIFF Well, why would I want to go to sleep if it was in the middle of the daytime?

MEL What about tablets?

GRIFF Oh yeah, I tried them and all.

MEL Well?

GRIFF There're eighteen in a pack.

MEL You want to think about something nice, think about that, something like Kim Basinger.

GRIFF What, Kim Basinger off the films?

MEL Yeah, the one with the bee-stung lips and in all that *9½ Weeks*.

GRIFF   Oh, yeah.

MEL   Well, you think about her coming along and creeping under your duvet, and think about getting in Kim Basinger and satisfying her.

GRIFF   I thought I was trying to get rid of my worries, not fret myself to death.

MEL   I tell you what, though, you worry too much. Look at me. I never worry about my career – I could take it or leave it. Money just doesn't bother me. Either I have it or I don't. Relationships, they come, they go, that's life. Life. And what am I?

GRIFF   You're an unemployed divorced bankrupt living in a Salvation Army hostel.

MEL   Yeah, but I sleep a lot, don't I?

KIDS

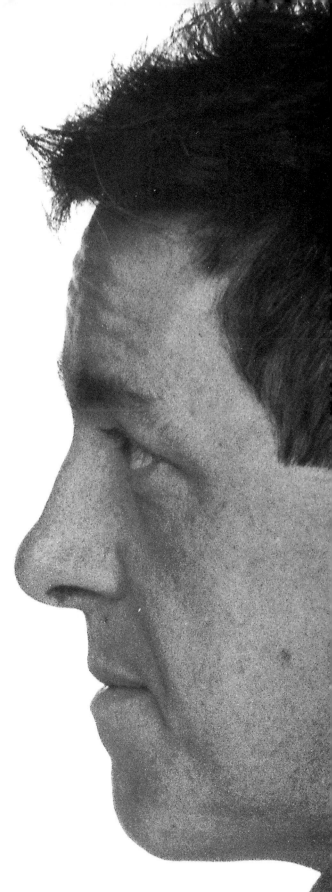

MEL   Tell you what is dreadful at the moment, though, it's that, er, drug stuff. That is awful. That's an awful, awful thing. It's an epidemic, isn't it, it's a, it's a canker in our society.

GRIFF   Yeah.

MEL   Rot in the fabric of the very society in which we live. If ever I thought any kid of mine was dabbling in drugs, I'd kill him.

GRIFF   Would you?

MEL   Yeah, kill him straight off, put him out of his misery. Drugs, wallop, that's the end of him.

GRIFF   What is it all about, though, what is it all about? What are they doing, the kids? They take this 'E' stuff, drink a couple of gallons of pineapple juice and bounce up and down in a shed all night.

MEL   Where's the pleasure in that? You'd think they'd have more sense.

GRIFF   What is it, then, that 'E'?

MEL   'E'? Ecstasy? Well, that's the trouble. No, nobody knows. They don't, they don't know what goes in it. It's what they call a designer drug.

GRIFF   What, Terence Conran takes it, does he?

MEL   No, no.

GRIFF   Well, what does it do, then?

MEL   Well, apparently it makes you a bit, you know, it makes you 'ooly-wooly, dunnit?

GRIFF   Yeah. 'Ooly-wooly?

MEL   Yeah.

GRIFF   It's that bad, then?

MEL   Oh, yeah.

GRIFF Is that entertaining, then, for them, being 'ooly-wooly?

MEL Well, if you like that sort of thing, it gives you the hallucination of wanting to touch people.

GRIFF Does it?

MEL Yeah. Apparently you take one of, one of these each, right, 'cos they come in all different sorts, these . . .

GRIFF Oh, yeah. I didn't know that.

MEL Well, yeah. You've got soft drugs, obviously. Soft ones. Then you've got the extra-soft ones, then you've got the absorbent and the super-strength ones.

GRIFF What, and does it make you want to touch people, you said, that 'E'? Touch people?

MEL Oh yeah, that's one of the side effects of the drug. Apparently the user gets an urge to fondle other people.

GRIFF Does he? Does he?

MEL Yeah, so they say, and 'cos he's a bit 'ooly-wooly he doesn't give a monkey's who he fondles, that's why they all go to these huge sheds, see? So there's plenty of other people to fondle.

GRIFF Yeah.

MEL I imagine there being a bit of hell to pay if you did it down the pub.

GRIFF So, is it like an aphr . . . aphranodisiac, this Ecstasy?

MEL No. No, there's no such thing as an aphranodisiac. I read that in an in-depth scientific study.

GRIFF What was that?

MEL *Penthouse*. What it does, is it releases your inhibitions. So, obviously in the normality of life there are certain formal restrictions on our behaviour, but when the drugs take hold, then, and you get a bit 'ooly-wooly, yeah, well, all bets are off, aren't they? People do all the things they wouldn't normally do.

GRIFF So, I might drive home from work via Ebury Street?

MEL Possibly. It'd be a bit, a bit more outrageous than that, though.

GRIFF Or how about an extra half a beer down the pub on Thursdays?

MEL Yeah, possibly.

GRIFF Or take over ten items through the express checkout at Tesco's?

MEL Possibly.

GRIFF Yeah, or park in a disabled space.

MEL Yeah, well, it'd be quite horrifying to see you out of your box, obviously.

GRIFF But, tell me this, 'cos I'm worried now. How can I tell if my little Donovan has been doing that stuff?

MEL The Ecstasy? Well, with that, with that it's easy. I mean, if your teenage kid suddenly seems to take a liking to you, he's probably on it. But, I mean, does he hang about with strange friends?

GRIFF I dunno. I dunno who he goes around with these days.

MEL Yeah, but, does he stay out, late at nights?

GRIFF Well, I'm not in much myself, so I can't really tell.

MEL Does he have bags under his eyes?

GRIFF I dunno, I haven't seen him for about six weeks.

MEL Yeah, well, it's very difficult being a parent . . .

GRIFF Oh, it is, very difficult. But what are you supposed to do with them, eh, kids, eh?

MEL I know, mate. You work and you slave, you put 'em, you put 'em through school, and then, then, they go all crazy on you. But in the end they come to their senses, don't they, they settle down at the age of about thirteen, and stick you in an old people's home. I mean, who's complaining? But let's face it, when we were kids, eh . . .

GRIFF Co-oo!

51

MEL   Teenagers?!

GRIFF   What!

MEL   Hey!

GRIFF   Hoo-oo!

MEL   Yeah!

GRIFF   Whoo-oof!

MEL   We sown a few wild oats in our time, haven't we, eh? We cut a rug!

GRIFF   Yeah!

MEL   Painted the town red!

GRIFF   Yeah!

MEL   Pushed the boat out!

GRIFF   Yeah!

MEL   We did have a funny load of holiday jobs, didn't we? But we did them, we had holiday jobs.

GRIFF   Yeah!

MEL   But look at that nephew of mine.

GRIFF   Brucie?

MEL   You know what he's got into? That ram-raiding.

GRIFF   Has he? He never has!

MEL   Yeah. He's just a learner. At the moment.

GRIFF   Well, how d'you mean?

MEL   Well, he still uses his own car. But, uh, well, it's terrible, isn't it? What they done to the insurance. Did you see that report in *Which Car?* Apparently the only one you can have round our area is a Saracen tank! But I blame the manufacturers. But, I mean, I'm no criminal, but there is no car, there is no car, that you can show me – maybe two or three – you show me all the cars, and there's only two or three that I couldn't get into. I mean, as long as I had the key obviously. But, I mean, what is happening, what is happening? There's some of them estates, they're no-go areas!

GRIFF   Well, how d'you mean?

MEL Well, nobody goes there. I mean, it's an epidemic. Nobody goes shopping any more. You daren't ask anyone to nip out and get you a packet of fags. I tell you, you say to some of them kids, 'Pop down the grocer's,' they go out, steal a car, smash through the window, pint of milk, loaf of bread and a couple of pounds of squashed tomatoes. It's ridiculous to blame the kids, though, isn't it? I blame the retail industry. They should keep proper hours. If the shops was open at one in the morning, none of this would happen.

GRIFF What is all that business! Round us they tried to brighten up the estate, it didn't do the slightest bit of good.

MEL They, you know, what did they do, then?

GRIFF Well, they put, you know, put some glass in the windows, removed a load of unsightly junk.

MEL What was that?

GRIFF The lift. I pity today's young people, there's no openings for them, is there?

MEL Except in the front of shops. Mind, look at old Harry the Hat's boy. He tried, but in the end he ended up, as they all do, doing the old ram-raiding. Last month he stole a Rolls-Royce, he did. He smashed it into the Citroën showroom and got away with a 2CV. So, then there was an 'orrific chase, and of course a tragedy ensued. He ended up dead. But there we are, you see. Of course on the estate, and Harry the Hat, they all claimed the police was out to get him, and they were. Just because he was a known criminal, the police were after him. I mean, really! Mind you, they gave him a good send-off.

GRIFF Did they?

MEL Yeah. They ram-raided the funeral parlour.

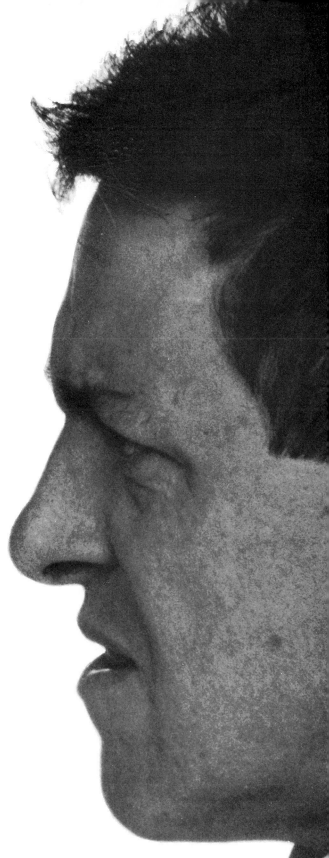

DOGS

GRIFF It's terrible trying to bring up a kid round my way, isn't it?

MEL Yeah.

GRIFF The graffiti on the walls, the broken windows, and the filth everywhere.

MEL Yeah, you really ought to get a cleaning woman or something.

GRIFF I mean, on the streets. The worst is all the dog mess all over the pavements.

MEL Yeah . . . I blame the owners.

GRIFF No, it's definitely the dogs.

MEL Yeah.

GRIFF They shouldn't be allowed in the cities. They should be banned, or there ought to be a huge licence fee.

MEL Ah, but, what about the poor old pensioners?

GRIFF No, people should be allowed to have a pensioner if they want to, but a dog is a different matter. You see, it's dangerous for the kiddies.

MEL Ah, but you've never been a doggy person. You don't see the positive side. I've always kept dogs myself. Do you remember old Tizer?

GRIFF Old Tizer, yes.

MEL Fantastic old dog, Tizer, a great dog, friendly, happy, a great character.

GRIFF He was a Rottweiler, wasn't he?

MEL Yeah . . . well, he was half Rottweiler, half poodle.

GRIFF He was a cross-breed?

MEL   He was a bloody angry breed – five stone of throbbing muscle, topped off with a little tail shaped like a pipe-cleaner.

GRIFF   He was a bit vicious, though, wasn't he?

MEL   Only when provoked.

GRIFF   Yeah, well, what provoked him?

MEL   Virtually anything, as it happens.

GRIFF   That's what I mean – these dogs are dangerous for the kids.

MEL   Ah, now, that is a complete fallacy.

GRIFF   Is it?

MEL   A huge violent dog need not be dangerous to children.

GRIFF   No?

MEL   Well, the Doberman I used to have, gentle as a lamb he was . . . What was his name?

GRIFF   Slasher.

MEL   Slasher, that was it. He wouldn't hurt a fly, he used to have kids riding on his back. He loved kids.

GRIFF   Well, he did eat the milkman's boy, didn't he?

MEL   Yeah, but, that was the kid's fault. If he'd just stood still . . .

GRIFF   He shouldn't have been playing football in the park, really, should he?

MEL   But the dog didn't know that, did he? Mind you, the dogs I've got now, my pit bulls. They are ferocious.

GRIFF   Are they?

MEL   Vicious.

GRIFF   Fergie and Di?

MEL   Fergie and Di . . . They're evil. I tell you, these dogs do not mess around. And once they decide to bite something, it stays bit.

GRIFF   Once bitten . . .

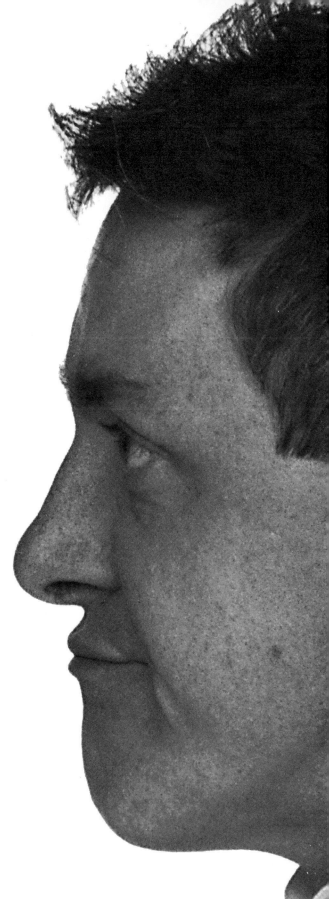

MEL Once bitten, always bitten . . . If either Fergie or Di clamps her jaws round your testicles, you can kiss goodbye to your wedding tackle.

GRIFF Either that or spend the rest of your life with a pit bull stuffed down your trousers.

MEL As a matter of fact, I'm thinking of breeding them.

GRIFF Are you? I think I'd like to see that.

MEL No, I mean breeding from them. 'Cos I'm thinking of getting into this dog-fight business.

GRIFF Dog-fights? It's cruel that, isn't it?

MEL Ah well, that's where you're so wrong. They love it. I went to see a dog-fight down Stratford way the other week, and in the first round there was a little Yorkshire Terrier, and he was up against this gigantic great bulldog. And, of course, this Yorkie didn't stand a chance. At the end its little jaw was hanging off, it was bleeding from head to foot, its fur was all pulled out, even his little tartan bow had snapped. But his little tail was still wagging.

GRIFF Was it?

MEL Yeah . . . It was in the other dog's mouth, but it was still wagging.

NATURE

MEL   Did you read about that Brigitte Bardot?

GRIFF   What's she been doing?

MEL   Well, apparently she's decided to leave all her money to her cats!

GRIFF   Has she?

MEL   Yeah.

GRIFF   Why's that?

MEL   Well, it's because she thinks that cats are more intelligent than human beings.

GRIFF   Well, they're certainly more intelligent than Brigitte Bardot, I can tell you that.

MEL   Mind you, it's good to have a pet, isn't it? Do you know, I went out the other day and bought myself a pink-legged tarantula.

GRIFF   Did you?

MEL   Yeah, called Edwina.

GRIFF   That's a spider, isn't it, a tarantula?

MEL   Yeah, it's big as a dinner plate, deadly poisonous, and covered in bristles.

GRIFF   Well, it's company for you, anyway.

MEL   Mind you, there's a bloke down our way, he collects them snakes and reptiles and things.

GRIFF   Does he?

MEL   Yeah. He's got, he's got a huge collection of all slivery things upstairs, that's what he's got, and his prize specimen's a seventy-two-foot boa-constrictor.

GRIFF   Well, that must take some looking after.

MEL   It does indeed, it does. 'Cos the other day, it escaped.

GRIFF   Did it?

MEL Yeah! And then they found it hiding in Mick Jagger's trousers.

GRIFF Must get a bit difficult to keep the things.

MEL Oh no, that's a myth.

GRIFF Is it?

MEL Oh yes, really very simple. They like to have a constant temperature, obviously, so, you know, I have to keep the central heating on, obviously.

GRIFF Yeah.

MEL And then they prefer it a little humid, so I put out little bowls of water all over the place, what makes it nice and steamy.

GRIFF Yeah.

MEL And obviously they require a diet of live insects. So I leave the carcass of a rotting antelope on the landing for a month or so now and again. Have you ever been down that Anita Roddick Body Shop thing?

GRIFF Oh yeah, I have, yeah, I get all my stuff down there.

MEL Do you?

GRIFF Yeah. Well, it's interesting, 'cos it's not tested on animals. So obviously I take it home and try it out on the dog first, but I get my jojoba and wild mountain raspberry shampoo from that, that Body Shop.

MEL That's all a bit exotic for me.

GRIFF Well, I like to think, you know, it's, it's a good idea, 'cos it's helping other people. 'Cos all these Third World people, they're selling their crops, right? They sell their jojoba crop, like, don't they, to that Anita Roddick. And all their, all their wild guavas and all that, and she buys up all that stuff, doesn't she? And it's all being made into potions for shop girls, isn't it? Guava shampoo . . .

MEL   Yeah.

GRIFF   But you see, the thing is now, she's bringing out the English version, 'cos of that sort of thought.

MEL   Oh yeah.

GRIFF   She's got the, er, brussel sprout body rub, cabbage shampoo, pea oil, fried egg conditioner, 'cos it's natural, isn't it, it's natural. I swear by it.

MEL   The fruits of the forest haemorrhoid cream. But she's made some money.

GRIFF   What would you do if you had Anita Roddick's money?

MEL   About ten years, I'd think.

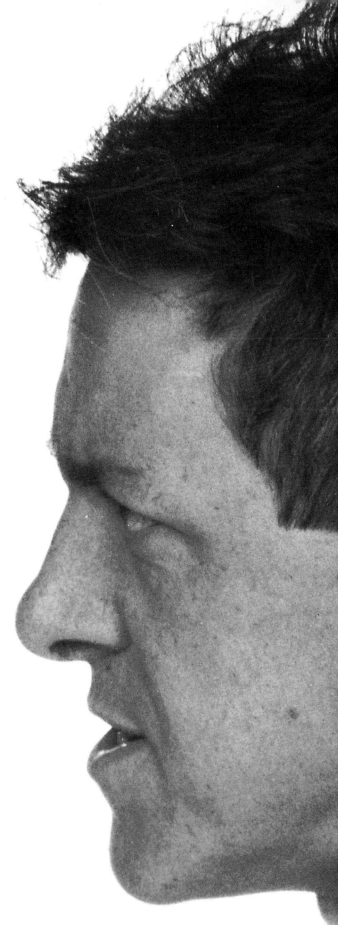

SATANIC RITUAL

GRIFF Isn't it terrible, though, about them satanic ritual things, in Epping Forest?

MEL Well, yes and no, 'cos as it happens, I am a warlock.

GRIFF Are you? I didn't know that.

MEL Yeah, I'm a lapsed warlock, obviously, but then I've always believed you don't have to go to a satanic abuse ritual to worship the Devil.

GRIFF 'Course. But do you go?

MEL Oh yeah, from time to time.

GRIFF How did you get involved in all this, then?

MEL Well, I got very disenchanted with organized religion, you know. I tried the Seventh Day Adventists, the Baptists, and working for IBM, but they all lacked a certain something.

GRIFF What was that?

MEL Well, not enough orgies, basically.

GRIFF Well, why do you always meet in Epping, then?

MEL Have you ever been to Epping? We meet on the seventh day of the seventh week of the seventh month.

GRIFF So, you don't meet very often. And, and why is that, then?

MEL Well, seven is a very significant number.

GRIFF Is it?

MEL Well, otherwise there wouldn't be any six or eight. We meet only, though, when the time is propitious.

GRIFF When is that?

MEL Well, when George gets a night off from the power station.

GRIFF Who's George?

MEL George is the Great White Witch of Essex, the Lord of Darkness, member of the most satanic order of the mighty Beelzebub, and he does a bit of French polishing on the side.

GRIFF Do you make sacrifices?

MEL Well, I don't go down the bowling as much as I used to.

GRIFF No, I mean, when it happens, do you make them sacrifices?

MEL Oh yes, yes, we do all, all the, all the doings, yes. Mmmn.

GRIFF So, what happens, then?

MEL Well, obviously we meet on a dark and stormy night, in the middle of Epping Forest. And we have to have a black cockerel, a black cockerel. 'Course, they're very difficult to get hold of these days, so we have to use the Grecian 2000, but it does a lovely job, and my job is to bite the head off the cockerel. The High Priestess collects the blood in the silver salver, and the Chief Warlock peels the potatoes and puts the oven on.

GRIFF I've heard terrible stories about things . . .

MEL Oh, you don't want to believe all that nonsense. Just because a group of people get together in the middle of the night in a clearing in Epping Forest and engage in ritual slaughter, people think there is something funny going on.

GRIFF So, are you a true believer?

MEL I am. But I'm afraid we've got a lot of people who are weekend satanists these days, you know. We got a load of people who only turn up for the satanic weddings and harvest festivals.

GRIFF So, if you're a real believer, you must know the number of the Beast?

MEL I do. Don't tell anybody, it's 071-631 3940, after six and at weekends.

INFLUENCES

MEL Did you see that programme the other day about Vera Lynn. Vera Lynn. Yeah, wasn't she marvellous. Yeah, she kept us going through the dark ages, didn't she?

GRIFF Who?

MEL Vera Lynn.

GRIFF What dark ages?

MEL The war, the Second World War.

GRIFF Oh yeah.

MEL Her and Winston Churchill. What a great man. He used to go on the radio and tell us not to worry. 'Never have so few owed so little for such a lot.' Marvellous. Yeah. Exactly. And then ole Vera, bless her, she'd get on the wireless too and she sang some marvellous songs.

GRIFF Yeah. 'There'll be blue birds over the White Cliffs of Dover', 'We'll meet again', 'Hitler, he only had one . . . '

MEL Yeah. Marvellous. She was an old trouper, Vera. Yeah, real old trouper.

GRIFF Yeah. I hate old troupers, don't you?

MEL Mind you, the most important thing about the war was the marvellous spirit, you see.

GRIFF Yeah.

MEL I mean, in those days you could walk your girlfriend home after the blackout, if you could find your way, and you didn't have to worry whether you were going to be mugged, whether you were going to be beaten up, the streets were safe. All you had to worry about was a bloody great bomb dropping on your head. And the Germans had Hitler, Goering, Goebbels . . .

GRIFF   Yeah, and we had John Mills, Noel Coward and David Niven.

MEL   But I'll tell you who's my idol. Sinatra.

GRIFF   Oh yeah.

MEL   He's got that indefinable something.

GRIFF   What's that?

MEL   Well, it's indefinable, isn't it? I like to think he's the one man who has had influence on my style.

GRIFF   What, you have dodgy relations with big-time criminals as well?

MEL   No, that's a rumour. Obviously a man in Frank's position is bound to rub shoulders with murderers and psychopaths from time to time. They only say it because he's Italian.

GRIFF   No, he's not Italian, he's American.

MEL   He was born in Jersey, of course, but originally he comes from a poor immigrant family of southern Italy, a family of ice-cream makers apparently, the Whippy's of Palermo. Mr Whippy went from street to street singing and selling toupés from a cart. Francis Albert Whippy had to fight his way to the top, he lived a life that's full, he travelled each and every byway . . .

GRIFF   Yeah, I've been in one of them minicabs.

MEL   Yeah. Marvellous songs. 'Start spreading the news, I'm leaving today . . . '

GRIFF   Yeah, well, don't go on my account.

MEL   Yeah, what about that other one: 'Unforgettable. Unforgettable, da da da da . . . ' No, that was Ole King Cole, of course. But he's played with all the greats, of course, Frank. Duke Wellington, the Jimmy Riddle Orchestra, Count Bassie, Shirley's dad, 'cos in the fifties he had a sort of gang.

GRIFF   Yeah, I've heard of them, the Six Pack.

MEL   The Rat Pack.

GRIFF   Who are they, then?

MEL   Oh, Dean Martin, Sammy Davies Junior, Alastair Cook, Michael Crawford and Kenny Lunch. What a bunch of guys. But he's the Governor, Frank, we call him the Boss.

GRIFF   Do you? Fancy him working down the depot.

JAZZ

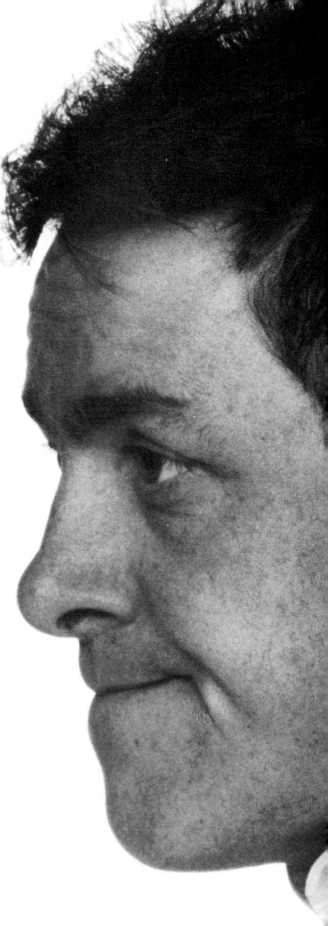

GRIFF Another year.

MEL Yeah.

GRIFF Dreadful year last year, wasn't it?

MEL Yeah. The Grim Reaper exacted a savage toll.

GRIFF Did he?

MEL Well, look at all the ones that went. Miles Davies . . .

GRIFF Isn't that a funny name, Miles.

MEL Yes, well, it's Scandinavian.

GRIFF Is it? What does it mean?

MEL 'A Long Way'.

GRIFF And Davies. What does that mean?

MEL Well, that means, 'To Tipperary'.

GRIFF I see. So his real name was, like, 'A Long Way To Tipperary'.

MEL Well, of course, 'cos that was his great number. Miles Davies plays 'A Long Way To Tipperary'.

GRIFF How did that go?

MEL It went . . . erm, like this. Blmmm, blmmm, blmmm, blmm etc, beep beep beep beep, etc.

GRIFF Oh yeah, that was good, wasn't it?

MEL Miles Davies could make that trumpet talk.

GRIFF That's clever. Could he make it play music?

MEL Not that I noticed. 'Course they've all gone now. Billie Holiday.

GRIFF What a great bloke, yeah. It's the drink and the drugs that do for them.

MEL And the dressing up in women's clothes.

GRIFF So, why do they do all that drinking and drugging, then?

MEL You have to be drunk to play music like that, don't you . . . blmm, blmm, blmmm. I'll tell you, if you're asking who is the greatest jazz player, the greatest jazz musician in the world, it's Acker Bilk.

GRIFF Yeah. He's the one what puts his bowler hat over the end of his instrument, isn't he?

MEL That's right, yeah. It's called a mute.

GRIFF Pity it doesn't work, isn't it?

MEL 'Cos, of course, that's how jazz started. It started in the streets of New Orleans. When groups of people would follow the funerals around.

GRIFF Who were they?

MEL Insurance salesmen.

GRIFF I see.

MEL They followed . . . they played the tunes, you see, and that's how all the jazz started.

'When the Saints
When the Saints
Go marching in
Oh when the Saints go marching in.'

GRIFF Yeah. And what's that other one . . . 'The Referee's a cunt, The Referee's a cunt . . . '

MEL Mind you, you can say what you like, but I think the greatest jazz giant that I ever clapped my eyes on must have been Buddy Rich. What a genius. I remember it must have been 1978 I went to see him gigging at the Albert Hall. Do you know, it's no kidding, he was the fastest drummer in the history of jazz. He was a blur, he got through his entire repertoire in thirty seconds flat and was on the eight-thirty flight back to New York.

DEBT

MEL I'm having a few problems.

GRIFF What, having trouble at the moment, mate, are you?

MEL Yeah. I'm trapped in a cycle of debt.

GRIFF Are you?

MEL I can't keep up the payments on me kid's Raleigh.

GRIFF Have you thought of killing yourself?

MEL I can't afford it. I am stripped to the bare essentials. I can't go on. I don't know what to do, I've got to eat, haven't I?

GRIFF Yeah, but you haven't got to eat at Mario's every night, have you?

MEL No, but . . . I'll do anything. Anything, anything.

GRIFF As long as it doesn't involve getting a job?

MEL No, that's not true. I went down the Peckham underpass the other day and done some of that cleaning the window-screen stuff.

GRIFF How did that go?

MEL Well, it didn't work, I chose the bus lane. Things have got so bad I'm thinking of selling my kidneys to Turkey. I went down the local hospital for an estimate.

GRIFF And?

MEL Well, it was good news and bad news. The good news, they were interested.

GRIFF What was the bad news?

MEL Only in a repair job.

GRIFF Have you thought of declaring yourself a bankrupt?

MEL Well, I'm not telling anybody, am I? That's the hidden cost, that is. It never hits the headlines. If you're in debt, you can't face your friends!

GRIFF What, because you owe them all money?

MEL No, because of the stigma.

GRIFF Well, everybody drives a cheap Japanese car these days.

MEL No, the social humiliation. I go in the pub, what sort of man am I, I can't buy my friends a round of drinks!

GRIFF You never did buy your friends a round of drinks!

MEL Listen, I'm staring disaster in the face, clinging on by my fingernails and scraping the bottom of the barrel.

GRIFF Well, at least you've got something to occupy yourself.

MEL I just need a helping hand up the ladder.

GRIFF You're not going stealing lead again, are you?

MEL Look, listen. Listen, look me in the face. Who is your best friend?

GRIFF My dog.

MEL No. There's absolutely nothing that I wouldn't do for you, you know.

GRIFF Except not ask me for money.

MEL I just need a little something to tide me over until the next payday.

GRIFF You haven't got a job!

MEL YOUR payday I'm talking about! Remember that time we were in Brighton. At the races, you needed money desperately, you, you, you, I didn't hesitate. I didn't think of anything, I gave it straight to you, straight away.

GRIFF No, I don't remember that.

MEL Oh no, that's right, it wasn't you. It was Big Harry.

GRIFF What, Big Harry, Chainsaw Harry, works as a bouncer down the Chinese gambling club?

MEL Yeah, but if it had been you, I'd have done the same, wouldn't I?

GRIFF What, if I'd been a bit bigger and had a chainsaw?

MEL Listen, I'll be absolutely straight with you. They've told me that if I don't give them four big ones by Thursday, they're gonna break my legs, and snap my fingers, and do me over something rotten.

GRIFF Who's this?

MEL The manager at Barclay's Bank. Listen, I'm desperate. I've gotta have four big ones.

GRIFF Four G?

MEL No, four K.

GRIFF What, you want me to give you four thousand quid?!

MEL Well, make it four thousand four hundred, and I can pay the dry-cleaning bill as well.

GRIFF I haven't got that sort of money, mate, I haven't got it!

MEL Well, you've got that car, you can sell that car!

GRIFF I can't just sell my car, what about my kids?

MEL Well, what d'your kids want the money for, they only spend it on gob-stoppers. Listen, I'm desperate, mate. I'm desperate. I'll end up in Cardboard City.

GRIFF You're not, you're not gonna move to Harlow Newtown?

MEL Listen, look at me. 'A friend in need is a friend indeed.'

GRIFF Mmmn. 'Neither a borrower nor a lender be.'

MEL 'Faith, hope and charity, and the greatest of these is charity.'

GRIFF 'Do not ask for credit, as refusal often offends.'

MEL 'Greater love hath no man that he should lay down his life for a friend.'

GRIFF 'You'll find a smarter investor at the Alliance & Leicester.'

MEL   Oh, it's hopeless, I'm wasting my time talking to you, what's the point?

GRIFF   Don't get upset. Look at it this way. Things may be bad now, two years from now you'll look back on these days and say, 'Those were the great days!'

AUSTRALIA

MEL I think I might emigrate to Australia . . .

GRIFF Oh no, don't do that, mate, don't do that.

MEL But it's a beautiful country . . . You can tell that when you're watching all the films and everything, can't you? What's that one with all the wild animals in the outback, what's it called . . . *Dingos Ate My Baby*, you know, it was in Australia, what was it called . . . er . . . Meryl Streep was in it . . .

GRIFF *Out of Africa*?

MEL That's the one, yeah.

GRIFF Yeah.

MEL That was absolutely beautiful. But don't you . . . honestly, don't you think I might . . . If I go out there, I might miss the culture?

GRIFF Oh yeah, definitely yeah.

MEL Yeah.

GRIFF What is that culture, then?

MEL Well, you see, in London you've got your opera, you got your ballets, you got your theatre, you got your concerts all on your doorstep, you see.

GRIFF What, in Peckham?

MEL Well, not in Peckham, but in London they're there, whereas in Australia you haven't got all that.

GRIFF No, you haven't. Well, you've got the ballet.

MEL They ain't got ballet in Australia!

GRIFF They have in Australia, yeah . . . Australian Rules, you know, but it is the ballet . . . But somehow I don't think there's any point in staying here just for the culture.

MEL Well, obviously . . .

GRIFF It's not the lack of culture what's gonna stop me going, you know, the ballet and all that.

MEL And then there's the spiders.

GRIFF What spiders, what spiders?

MEL In Australia they have some of the most deadliest spiders what is known to man.

GRIFF The deadliest spiders what is known to man?

MEL Yeah, the worst is the Sydney Funnyweb. I tell you, mate, if that bites you there is no anecdote, absolutely none. One bite, whoosh . . . end of story.

GRIFF Oh yeah. And what, where is this?

MEL You know where it lives?

GRIFF Well, in Australia.

MEL In the carsey.

GRIFF The deadliest spider known to man lives in the carsey?

MEL Lives in the carsey, mate.

GRIFF Well, I dunno . . .

MEL It sits there under the toilet seat with its seventeen eyes out on stalks . . . waiting and waiting . . . and you come in and drop your pants, you sit on the seat and snap! It's got you. It's got you.

GRIFF Snap!

MEL Snap!

GRIFF What, right on your didgeridoos?

MEL Yes. Bang on your billabong. And I tell you, mate, I tell you what, mate, from that moment the old todger starts to swell to five times its normal size.

GRIFF Does it?

MEL And you've only got ten minutes to live. Well, it's an agonizing choice, isn't it.

GRIFF I should think it is.

MEL I mean, do you spend the last ten minutes of your life, you know, sort of running around like a headless chicken seeking medical assistance, or do you put on your posing pouch and parade along Bondi hoping to go out in a blaze of glory?

HYPOCHONDRIA

MEL   I'm done for. I am not much longer for this world.
        My number's up.

GRIFF What, you mean you're ill?

MEL   Yes, yes, I'm ill.

GRIFF I didn't know you were sick. I mean, you look
        terrible, but I didn't know you were sick. You
        always look terrible, don't you.

MEL   Well, you know those pains I've been getting in
        my back . . .

GRIFF No.

MEL   Well, I've been getting these pains in my back
        and they have diagnosed them now as . . .
        twinges.

GRIFF Twinges? Fatal twinges, is that right? Is that what
        you've got, yeah?

MEL   Twinges, twinges coupled with shooting pains,
        tremulous palpitations and chronic drowsiness.

GRIFF You ought to see a doctor, then.

MEL   I have seen a doctor.

GRIFF Oh yeah.

MEL   I went down the Health Centre. I saw Frobisher.

GRIFF What did he say?

MEL   He said, he said he couldn't help me.

GRIFF He's a terrible doctor, isn't he?

MEL   Lousy.

GRIFF What's, what's he . . . he's no good at all.

MEL   Lousy, lousy.

GRIFF Is that all he said. I mean, you should have asked
        for a second opinion.

MEL   Well, I did.

GRIFF   And?

MEL   He said I was a work-shy layabout.

GRIFF   Well, that's another way of looking at it, I
suppose. Is that all?

MEL   He did, he did all the usual stuff: he told me to
give up smoking and all the rest . . .

GRIFF   Oh yeah. Did you?

MEL   Well, while he was examining me, yeah. Well, I
mean, it's ridiculous, isn't it, I mean, eight years at
medical school drinking all those gallons of beer
and playing rugby and that's the best they can
come up with.

GRIFF   I know, give up smoking. What do they know?

MEL   They don't know nothing, these doctors. Anyway,
I ended up . . . I went down to the new surgery at
the bottom of the hill and I saw the doctor there,
he's a nice bloke, Doctor, um, Doctor Locum. I
said to him straight, I said to him straight, 'Doc,
how long have I got?'

GRIFF   And what did he say?

MEL   Two minutes.

GRIFF   Two minutes?

MEL   Well, the surgery was full, I mean, there were
hundreds of people waiting to see him. Anyway,
he's sending me for some tests.

GRIFF   Not tests.

MEL   Yeah, you know, with a specialist.

GRIFF   What, a specialist in twinges?

MEL   A specialist. Well, I mean, apparently the top
man.

GRIFF   Well, that's the worst thing you can possibly hear,
isn't it? Isn't it, eh?

MEL   Why?

GRIFF Well, you go to see the top man, think about it, they're not going to get old Sir Willoughby Whatsisname off the golf course just to look at any old rubbish, are they? You've got something dreadful wrong with you. You're doomed, mate, you're doomed! I mean, where are you going?

MEL Peckham General.

GRIFF Not Peckham General! Not Peckham General.

MEL Peckham General. What's wrong with Peckham . . . ?

GRIFF Listen, listen, mate, right, my brother-in-law, right, he tells me that Peckham General is the filthiest hospital in the country.

MEL What does your brother-in-law know about it?

GRIFF He's the head cleaner.

MEL Oh.

GRIFF I wouldn't go in Peckham General if you paid me!

MEL Well, they did pay you – you was a porter there for four years.

GRIFF But I didn't go in there, did I?

MEL No, no, you didn't, that's true.

GRIFF No, I tell you, mate, whatever you do, whatever you do, they'll be all right, but if they tell you, right, they're putting you on Primrose Ward, don't go there. Don't go there! Don't go there.

MEL Why not?

GRIFF That Primrose Ward – Death Row, mate. Nobody ever comes out of Primrose Ward alive.

MEL What, nobody?

GRIFF Well, some of the nurses, occasionally, yes. But that's the holding bay for the mortuary, Primrose Ward.

MEL Hold on a minute, I'm only going there for a scan.

GRIFF Not a scan!

MEL There's nothing wrong with a scan.

GRIFF Oh my . . . No, go for the Barium Meal, mate, it's a bit easier. Go for the Barium Meal.

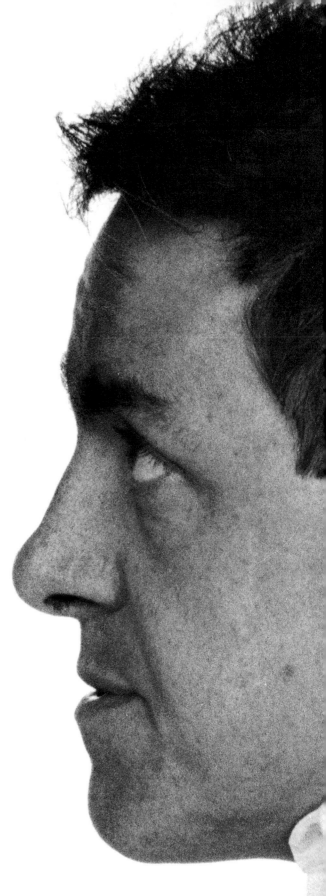

MEL How do you know about it?

GRIFF Well, I've had more Barium Meals than you've had hot dinners, I tell you.

MEL Yeah, but with that Barium Meal you have to drink all that nasty horrible white gluck stuff, don't you. Yergh, it's horrible that.

GRIFF Well, it's a treat after the hospital food, mate, I can tell you. It's a little bit of a problem you know, like, with the other, you know, when it, you know, when it comes out the other end, sort of thing, you know.

MEL Why?

GRIFF Well, it goes in like liquid clay and comes out like a sixty-two-piece earthenware tea-set.

MEL What if you've got constipation?

GRIFF Well, then you've got an early Henry Moore on your hands, ain't you?

REINCARNATION

MEL Medical science, eh? Man has practically cheated death.

GRIFF Has he?

MEL Oh yeah, but it's a two-edged sword.

GRIFF I didn't know that.

MEL These days they keep them going artificially. Take my Aunty Flo, she lost one of her lungs.

GRIFF Oh, silly old dear, always leaving things lying around aren't they?

MEL No, she lost the use of it. It folded up on her, she was at death's door, her lungs down, both her legs gone, completely gaga, done for. But would they turn off the life-support system? 'Course they wouldn't. They wouldn't even sack her from the Post Office. But these old dears.

GRIFF But what about my Uncle Leddy. He's still alive, but only by the skin of his teeth. He had that by-pass surgery.

MEL Cor, that can be dodgy, that one.

GRIFF Yeah, well, he had his appendix out on the Hanger Lane gyratory system. Terrible business. Apparently he was technically dead for three minutes and then they brought him back.

MEL That must have been a shock.

GRIFF Well, it was for me sister, she'd already cashed up on the life insurance.

MEL But if I was going to live for a few months, I'd want to know, wouldn't I, before it happens, like. Because there are so many things that I'd like to do that I've never done.

GRIFF What, wash your armpits?

MEL   Like travel. There are so many places I've never been.

GRIFF   Like where?

MEL   Well, like Hemel Hempstead.

GRIFF   I've never been there.

MEL   Yeah, you'd be ready for death after that I should think.

GRIFF   The Thames Barrier, that's another one.

MEL   Yeah, but don't you want to see the Taj Mahal by moonlight?

GRIFF   Never again, I was throwing up one of their curries in the gutter outside it only a couple of weeks ago.

MEL   Funny you should say that 'cos I had a curry the other day, it was one of them southern Indian ones.

GRIFF   Southern Indian ones? You mean, down Croydon way?

MEL   That's right, and they served up my curry and do you know what was there, right in the middle of my curry?

GRIFF   What?

MEL   A sultana.

GRIFF   A sultana in the middle of your curry?

MEL   A sultana. Right in the middle of my curry.

GRIFF   Was it dead?

MEL   Well, it was lying on its back with its legs in the air. But then these Indians, they have a funny attitude to death.

GRIFF   Do they?

MEL   Have you ever thought about reincarnation?

GRIFF   Come again.

MEL   I mean, reincarnation. Have you ever thought about it?

GRIFF   I don't believe that God exists like some old age pensioner.

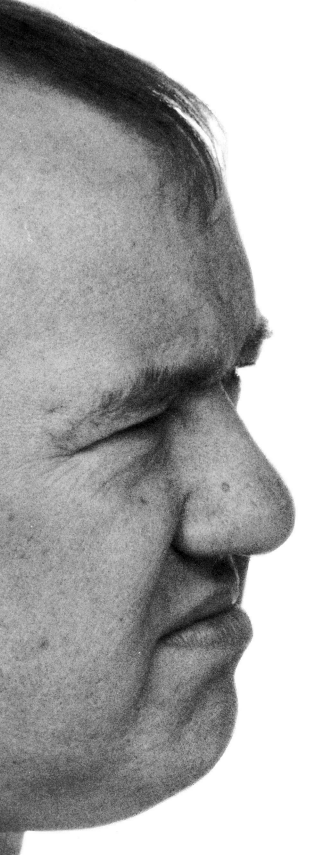

MEL But it stands to reason that there are things that are irrational which are sort of like being, sort of thing, I mean, you have just got to accept that there are some things that cannot be explained . . .

GRIFF Well, not by you obviously.

MEL Not by anybody. I'm talking about the big questions.

GRIFF What big questions?

MEL Universal questions to which there are no answers. Where do we come from?

GRIFF Peckham.

MEL Where are we going?

GRIFF I'm going to Peckham, I don't know about you.

MEL What are we doing here?

GRIFF Yeah, well, there are some questions you can't answer, obviously.

MEL But when you die, where do you think you'll go?

GRIFF Well, I'll go to the Co-op probably, they did my Granddad proud.

MEL No, I'm talking about the reincarnation. About being something. Well, I would like to be a racehorse, Arkle, Dancing Brave, Shergar. Yeah, I mean all you'd have to do is run a few races with a midget on your back, then you get all the food you want tied to your face in a bag.

GRIFF I can see why you'd like that. But personally if I was going to come back, I'd rather come back as a dragonfly.

MEL A dragonfly, what's the point of that?

GRIFF If you're a dragonfly, right, you only live for a day.

MEL Well, that's not much of a life, is it?

GRIFF   Ah, that's where you're wrong, it was on this
        programme, 'That's Life on Earth'. This dragonfly
        emerges from its pupil, dries out in the sun,
        flutter flutter; drinks some nectar, slurp slurp; and
        then he cops the nearest lady dragonfly, cop cop,
        and his eyes come out on stalks, or maybe they
        was out on stalks already, I don't remember . . .
        Anyway he doesn't hang about, he doesn't need
        a gin and tonic and a meal down the Chinky.
        It's straight aboard and he shags her until her eyes
        pop out. And that is his complete day, erk erk,
        flutter flutter, slurp slurp, shag shag. It's like a
        holiday in Ibiza.

MEL   Yeah, but then you die. One day is a bit short for
        a whole lifetime.

GRIFF   Ah, but that's where you're wrong, because
        under the reincarnation system you come straight
        back again as another dragonfly, erk erk, flutter
        flutter, slurp slurp, shag shag. And so on until the
        end of time. Bliss.

MEL   Well, that's typical, you haven't understood the
        entire idea of reincarnation at all. You've got no
        clue. There's no guarantee you'd come back as a
        dragonfly, you might come back as a . . . well, as
        a dung beetle.

GRIFF   How's that going to happen?

MEL   Well, obviously, if you weren't a good dragonfly
        the first time round.

GRIFF   Do me a favour, how can you be a bad dragonfly?

MEL   It's obvious. You come back, you don't know
        you've only got one day, you're worn out with
        the erk erk; you think, never mind the slurping
        and the shagging, I'll do that tomorrow, yeah.
        But talking of language, do you know what the
        commonest word in English is?

GRIFF   Fucking hell, that's fucking difficult. The
        commonest fucking word in the English fucking
        language? Oh fuck me, it's not vicar, is it?

MEL No, what is the commonest word used, like, the most frequent?

GRIFF Is it 'E'?

MEL Good guess, but wrong.

GRIFF 'A'?

MEL Good guess, but wrong.

GRIFF 'I'?

MEL Good guess, but wrong.

GRIFF Yes.

MEL Good guess, but wrong.

GRIFF Well, I've got a pretty good idea now. It's not 'Good guess but wrong', is it?

MEL But it's the mystery of language. For example, did you know your average man has got a vocabulary of about twenty thousand words?

GRIFF That's incredible. What's a vocabulary?

MEL Well, it's the words a person uses.

GRIFF Well, when you put it like that, I can see what you're talking about. So I use twenty thousand words?

MEL Well, you, yeah, you might not have as many as that.

GRIFF Well, how many do I use?

MEL About a hundred and thirty.

GRIFF Listen, mate, my vocabulary is absolutely big.

MEL I don't think so, mate.

GRIFF Let's count up how many words I know, then.

MEL Come on.

GRIFF Well, that's two for a start, isn't it. Come on. What else? That's another two. What else?

MEL So we've got so far 'come on', 'what', and 'what else'. That's four.

GRIFF Four is one.

MEL That's five.

GRIFF Five is one.

MEL   That's six.
GRIFF   Six is one.
MEL   That's seven.
GRIFF   Seven is one.
MEL   That's eight.
GRIFF   Eight is one.
MEL   That's nine.

DIVORCE

MEL I'm sorry I haven't been my usual self recently, mate.

GRIFF That's all right. No need to apologize for that.

MEL No, I've been going through a very miserable and expensive time.

GRIFF What, you've renewed your Arsenal season ticket, have you?

MEL No. My divorce came through. Take it from me, divorce is an appalling event for anybody. I don't care who they are, old or young, male or female . . .

GRIFF Married or single . . .

MEL Of course, it's the children I feel sorriest for.

GRIFF Yeah, well, they shouldn't get married so young, should they?

MEL I'm talking about the children of the marriage. Of course, that was part of the trouble between me and Cheryl. She always wanted children and, well, I . . .

GRIFF You wanted barmaids.

MEL Yeah.

GRIFF So whose fault was it that you and Cheryl split up?

MEL Well, it's not a question of fault, really. After all it takes two to tango, doesn't it?

GRIFF Yeah, and eight to do an eightsome reel.

MEL Eh? No, with me and Cherry, it was six of one, half a dozen of the other.

GRIFF   In your case it was mainly the other . . . and more than six some weeks.

MEL   Yeah. Yeah. We were both equally to blame. She was at fault for her nagging, her jealousy and for being such a slut around the house. And I was at fault for marrying the stupid bitch in the first place.

GRIFF   Did you divorce her, then?

MEL   No, she divorced me. I don't know why, really. I mean, I gave her a good home, didn't I?

GRIFF   That council flat you had?

MEL   Yeah, that's the one.

GRIFF   She had that before you moved in, didn't she?

MEL   She used to go into a frenzy if I so much as looked at another woman.

GRIFF   Well, you go in a frenzy if you so much as look at another woman.

MEL   I tell you, she was even jealous of me and Nellie.

GRIFF   Not Smellie Nellie, the fat bird down the Goat and Anchor?

MEL   Yeah.

GRIFF   Corfhhhh!

MEL   Her mum, she was jealous of her.

GRIFF   Never!

MEL   And your Aunt Madge.

GRIFF   No!

MEL   I kid you not . . . and those were just the ones I did have it off with. Anyway, that's all behind me now. We've had one of these 'quickie' divorces.

GRIFF   How long did it take, then?

MEL   Four years. But it's so degrading. Having to wash all your dirty linen in public.

GRIFF   Yeah. You have to go down the launderette now, then, do you?

MEL Yeah, but, you know what it's like. It's going to be difficult to accept that I am going to be responsible for the life of a whole new human being as a result of a single desperate act of coupling in one night of passion.

GRIFF But you were living with Cheryl for five years.

MEL Yeah, but obviously only one night of passion produced a baby. Anyway, I've faced up to my responsibilities now, haven't I? I knew my attitude could never be the same again when I looked into that face with the clear blue eyes, the big puffy cheeks, the little wispy strands of hair.

GRIFF That was the face of your little baby?

MEL No, it was the face of the judge who done the paternity suite. Seven pounds fifty a week I have to pay Cheryl for her to spend on the baby.

GRIFF Seven pound fifty a week to bring up a baby?

MEL Yeah, well, it sounds a lot but I wouldn't expect her to give me anything back, anything left over, no. I don't mind her treating herself to a few luxuries. She's never wasted money, Cheryl, I'll give her that.

GRIFF Do you give her the seven fifty?

MEL Well, not yet, no. Blimey, the Judge only made the order six months ago. I haven't been back to the Court for non-payment and arrears and all that yet. You've got to do things in the proper order. But I won't see the kid starve.

GRIFF Well, you never see the kid at all, do you?

MEL Of course I do. I saw him yesterday. I look at that little baby, my son, and I think that he has got the possibilities, or the potential to become anything. He could be an artist, a scientist, he could play for England, he could grow up to be a soldier or a sailor, a tinker or a tailor or a candlestick-maker, a butcher, a baker, yeah, he could become the man who reads out the regional news after the News at Ten. He could become a traffic warden, a train driver, someone who has to climb up and clean the windows on very tall buildings. He could sell double glazing . . .

GRIFF   Or he could become a complete piss artist like his father.

LOVE

MEL I think I'm in love! I'm talking about love, I'm talking about love, mate. Oh, I wish you could see her. She's such a beautiful young thing.

GRIFF Is she? How do you mean young?

MEL Well, she's seventeen.

GRIFF Seventeen?

MEL Yeah, well, she looks seventeen. You can't tell these days, can you, to be quite honest. I mean, she might be thirty-six, but I don't care. When I hear her name it's like a thousand violins shimmering across the clear blue waters of the Aegean.

GRIFF Yeah. What's her name?

MEL Tony.

GRIFF That's a bloke's name, isn't it?

MEL No. Tony, it's an abbreviation. It's Tony for short.

GRIFF Oh, what's it long for, then?

MEL It's Anthony. There's music to my ears, her name. Tony, Tony, Tony, Tony. I've got it bad, haven't I?

GRIFF You've got it terrible by the sound of it, yeah.

MEL Yeah, but you do soppy things when you're in love, don't you?

GRIFF You do, yeah.

MEL Walking in the rain, and wishing on a star.

GRIFF And throwing the cat in the canal. Well, that was a soppy thing. Well, it was when we dragged it out anyway, yeah.

MEL You know what I found myself doing the other day?

GRIFF What's that, then?

MEL I found myself writing a poem.

GRIFF A poem! You didn't, did you! Come on, how'd it go, then?

MEL No, I . . .

GRIFF Go on, how'd it go, how'd it go?

MEL All right then, OK.

> There was an old man of Darjeeling,
> Whose todger stretched up to the ceiling
> It said on the door
> Don't spit on the floor,
> So he carefully spat on my Tony.

GRIFF You've got it bad, there's no doubt about that. I mean, tell me, are you thinking of tying the knot?

MEL I don't think so, 'cos we might want babies later.

GRIFF You are going to get married, then?

MEL Oh, I think all in due course. But, you see, at the moment we've both been through very stressful, very traumatic periods. I've been through the divorce with Sharon, getting custody of the kids and everything . . .

GRIFF And what about Tony?

MEL Well, she's been taking her GCSEs.

GRIFF She is seventeen, isn't she? I mean far be it from me to say . . .

MEL What what what?

GRIFF I mean, it's none of my business . . .

MEL Well, what?

GRIFF What's she like in bed?

MEL Well, can I describe the sun, the moon and the stars all rolled into one?

GRIFF I doubt it. I mean, you've got to think, you see . . . Listen, can I speak to you as one intelligent human being to another?

MEL You can give it a whirl, yeah.

GRIFF I mean, you know . . . What was it, only three weeks ago you was head-over-heels in love with that trampoline artist, weren't you?

MEL Well, so?

GRIFF Yeah, well, are you sure this is not just happening on the rebound?

MEL No, I'm in love, I'm in love with her.

GRIFF You've got to see it from her point of . . . I mean, you're old enough to be her old man, aren't you?

MEL What are you trying to say?

GRIFF Well, look, she's seventeen, right? She's young, she's an impressionable young girl, she don't know what's going on in the world . . .

MEL Right, yeah.

GRIFF And along comes an older, cleverer, more mature, sophisticated man and turns her head.

MEL Well, so?

GRIFF Well, it could happen.

IMPOTENCE

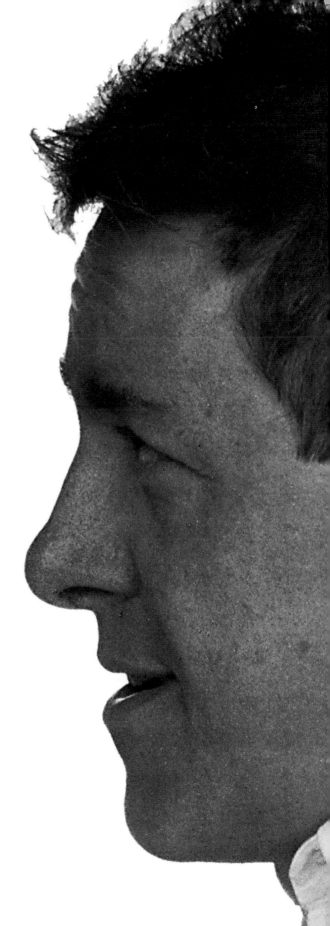

GRIFF Do you mind if I ask you a bit of advice?

MEL Of course not.

GRIFF I've been having a bit of trouble in the old southern region.

MEL Have you thought about taking the bus?

GRIFF No, I mean, down there.

MEL Oh, down there, I see. Well, what is it?

GRIFF It's that thing that dangles between your legs.

MEL Well, I know that but what's the problem?

GRIFF That is the problem, it just dangles. I'm having a bit of trouble with the old, er . . .

MEL A bit of impotence in the old, er . . .

GRIFF Yes, it's gone on extended leave. It's no use to man nor beast.

MEL Well, yes, I can see it's a problem. It's a very personal thing. Have you discussed it with your partner?

GRIFF What, Ted? He can't even look after his half of the stall.

MEL No, no. I'm talking about your sleeping partner. Have you mentioned it to your wife? Have you told her that you're impotent?

GRIFF Well, I didn't need to tell her, did I? It stuck out a mile. I mean, it didn't stick out a mile, it was awful. But she's done her best, she's been very helpful.

MEL Well, she's a brick, isn't she?

GRIFF She is, she's a tower of strength. She went out and got one of them sexy outfits – a French maid thing, it was, with a little pinafore thing . . . It was really offputting. And then she cooked me my favourite dinner.

MEL What, toad in the hole?

GRIFF No, I've gone off that. And after dinner, she turned the lights down low and she said to me, 'Come on, darling, let's see if we can work that old magic again. But get a move on because I've got to go down the Bingo in half an hour.'

MEL And, er . . . any luck?

GRIFF She got twenty-five quid on a bonus card and five pounds off a carriage clock.

MEL Yeah, you see, to be honest, mate, what I think you've got to do is go and see a specialist.

GRIFF No, I'd be too embarrassed.

MEL No, honestly, that's what I did. I went to see the doctor.

GRIFF Did you? Did you have this trouble?

MEL Yes, I had this trouble for several months.

GRIFF And what happened?

MEL Well, I went to see the doctor and, of course, wouldn't you know it, I mean, you go and see the doctor and suddenly everything's OK again.

GRIFF Well, that sounds a bit embarrassing.

MEL Well, it was. I was standing there in the doctor's surgery and I dropped me kecks and it's on duty.

GRIFF What did the doctor say?

MEL Well, she was very understanding . . .

DRUGS

MEL   Took out a video of *Midnight Express* last night.

GRIFF   Oh right, yeah.

MEL   Terrifying. Horrendous. Three pounds fifty a night.

GRIFF   What happens in that?

MEL   Well, it's about a bloke. He's smuggling drugs out of Turkey and he's put in jail for life. Dope.

GRIFF   He was to get caught, wasn't he, really.

MEL   No, dope is what he was smuggling out.

GRIFF   Oh right, yeah.

MEL   Hashish.

GRIFF   Where was he taking it?

MEL   He was taking it to the States.

GRIFF   What was he going to do with it there?

MEL   He was going to peddle it.

GRIFF   I thought you smoked it.

MEL   After you've peddled it.

GRIFF   Oh right, yeah. So, like a bicycle.

MEL   No. Pushing it.

GRIFF   So, you do a little peddling then you get off and you push it.

MEL   All right.

GRIFF   It's terrible, isn't it, all those drug pushers. I think they're the scum on the backside of humanity.

MEL   You can always tell a drug pusher.

GRIFF   How's that?

MEL   They look just like you and me. But there's a certain something that gives them away.

GRIFF   What is that?

MEL   It's the way they come up to you and ask you if you want any drugs.

GRIFF   It's terrible that Paul McCartney thing, isn't it?

MEL   What was he doing? Going through Customs and getting pinched by the Nips.

GRIFF   It's painful when that happens.

MEL   He was busted by the Japanese.

GRIFF   Why does he do that? He writes all those lovely little songs and he's got all the money and he lives on the farm with all his sheep and he's married to that Linda, isn't he? He only takes them as a social thing, doesn't he? Takes them like his cannabis or his gin and tonic.

MEL   One thing will lead to another. There's a little kid round my way. This is a very sad story. He started off on the extra strong mints. Then he was sniffing the inside of the coffee grinder, then it was the glue, then it was the pills and finally smack.

GRIFF   His dad fixed him one round here.

MEL   Smack. Smack, the big E.

GRIFF   The big E?

MEL   ERoin. It's claimed a lot of people. Terrible. Back in the sixties . . . lot of pop stars. Jimi, Janice. . . .

GRIFF   Jimi who?

MEL   Jimi Hendrix. Lenny . . .

GRIFF   Janice who?

MEL   Janice Joplin. You know, me and Bobby McGee.

GRIFF   You and all, then?

MEL   Lenny . . . Bruce.

GRIFF   Both of them. Sammy. He got done for drugs, didn't he?

MEL   Sammy who?

GRIFF   Sammy Patel. The chemist.

MEL   Nowadays it's all the rage for this cocaine. It's rife amongst the nobs, mate.

GRIFF   Well, I thought you took it up your nose.

HOW TO WRITE YOUR OWN
HEADTOHEAD

1. Wake up late.
2. Linger over breakfast, toying with ideas for your hilarious Head to Head.
3. Put it off 'til tomorrow.
4. Repeat stages 1–3 as often as seems appropriate.
5. Make coffee in industrial quantities.
6. Sit at desk, turn on computer, write 'Head to Head' at top of page.
7. Read the paper.
8. Phone all your friends.
9. Eventually find someone to go to lunch with.
10. Return as late as possible, depressed.
11. Walk around a bit.
12. Sigh a lot.
13. Mutter.
14. Sob.
15. Write the Head to Head.